An Analysis of

Sheila Fitzpatrick's

Everyday Stalinism
Ordinary Life in Extraordinary
Times: Soviet Russia in the 1930s

Victor Petrov
with
Riley Quinn

www.macat.com
info@macat.com

Cover illustration: Etienne Gilfillan

Cataloguing in Publication Data
A catalogue record for this book is available from the British Library.
Library of Congress Cataloguing-in-Publication Data is available upon request.

ISBN 978-1-912302-54-3 (hardback)
ISBN 978-1-912128-10-5 (paperback)
ISBN 978-1-912281-42-8 (e-book)

Notice
The information in this book is designed to orientate readers of the work under analysis,
to elucidate and contextualise its key ideas and themes, and to aid in the development
of critical thinking skills. It is not meant to be used, nor should it be used, as a
substitute for original thinking or in place of original writing or research. References and
notes are provided for informational purposes and their presence does not constitute
endorsement of the information or opinions therein. This book is presented solely for
educational purposes. It is sold on the understanding that the publisher is not engaged
to provide any scholarly advice. The publisher has made every effort to ensure that
this book is accurate and up-to-date, but makes no warranties or representations with
regard to the completeness or reliability of the information it contains. The information
and the opinions provided herein are not guaranteed or warranted to produce particular
results and may not be suitable for students of every ability. The publisher shall not be
liable for any loss, damage or disruption arising from any errors or omissions, or from
the use of this book, including, but not limited to, special, incidental, consequential or
other damages caused, or alleged to have been caused, directly or indirectly, by the
information contained within.

CONTENTS

THE MACAT LIBRARY

The Macat Library is a series of unique academic explorations of seminal works in the humanities and social sciences – books and papers that have had a significant and widely recognised impact on their disciplines. It has been created to serve as much more than just a summary of what lies between the covers of a great book. It illuminates and explores the influences on, ideas of, and impact of that book. Our goal is to offer a learning resource that encourages critical thinking and fosters a better, deeper understanding of important ideas.

Each publication is divided into three Sections: Influences, Ideas, and Impact. Each Section has four Modules. These explore every important facet of the work, and the responses to it.

This Section-Module structure makes a Macat Library book easy to use, but it has another important feature. Because each Macat book is written to the same format, it is possible (and encouraged!) to cross-reference multiple Macat books along the same lines of inquiry or research. This allows the reader to open up interesting interdisciplinary pathways.

To further aid your reading, lists of glossary terms and people mentioned are included at the end of this book (these are indicated by an asterisk [*] throughout) – as well as a list of works cited.

Macat has worked with the University of Cambridge to identify the elements of critical thinking and understand the ways in which six different skills combine to enable effective thinking.
Three allow us to fully understand a problem; three more give us the tools to solve it. Together, these six skills make up the **PACIER** model of critical thinking. They are:

ANALYSIS – understanding how an argument is built
EVALUATION – exploring the strengths and weaknesses of an argument
INTERPRETATION – understanding issues of meaning

CREATIVE THINKING – coming up with new ideas and fresh connections
PROBLEM-SOLVING – producing strong solutions
REASONING – creating strong arguments

To find out more, visit **WWW.MACAT.COM.**

CRITICAL THINKING AND *EVERYDAY STALINISM*

Primary critical thinking skill: REASONING
Secondary critical thinking skill: EVALUATION

How was the Soviet Union like a soup kitchen? In this important and highly revisionist work, historian Sheila Fitzpatrick explains that a reimagining of the Communist state as a provider of goods for the 'deserving poor' can be seen as a powerful metaphor for understanding Soviet life as a whole. By positioning the state both as a provider and as a relief agency, Fitzpatrick establishes it as not so much a prison (the metaphor favoured by many of her predecessors), but more the agency that made possible a way of life.

Fitzpatrick's real claim to originality, however, is to look at the relationship between the all-powerful totalitarian government and its own people from both sides – and to demonstrate that the Soviet people were not totally devoid of either agency or resources. Rather, they successfully developed practices that helped them to navigate everyday life at a time of considerable danger and multiple shortages. For many, Fitzpatrick shows, becoming an informer and reporting fellow citizens – even family and friends – to the state was a successful survival strategy.

Fitzpatrick's work is noted mainly as an example of the critical thinking skill of reasoning; she marshals evidence and arguments to deliver a highly persuasive revisionist description of everyday life in Soviet time. However, her book has been criticized for the way in which it deals with possible counter-arguments, not least the charge that many of the interviewees on whose experiences she bases much of her analysis were not typical products of the Soviet system.

ABOUT THE AUTHOR OF THE ORIGINAL WORK

The historian **Sheila Fitzpatrick** was born in Australia in 1941. She grew up with a socialist father who supported the aims of the Russian Revolution (though not how things worked out afterward), and inspired her to concern herself with the lives of ordinary people. Fitzpatrick brought this mindset to her scholarship, where she specialized in the history of the Soviet Union, looking at it through the eyes of peasants and workers. After spending much of her career in the United States, Fitzpatrick has returned to Australia, where she currently teaches at the University of Sydney.

ABOUT THE AUTHORS OF THE ANALYSIS

Victor Petrov is a PhD candidate in Modern European history at Columbia University, where his research focuses on Eastern Europe. He received his BA (2009) and M.Phil.(2011) in Modern History from Oxford University.

Riley Quinn holds master's degrees in politics and international relations from both LSE and the University of Oxford.

ABOUT MACAT

GREAT WORKS FOR CRITICAL THINKING

Macat is focused on making the ideas of the world's great thinkers accessible and comprehensible to everybody, everywhere, in ways that promote the development of enhanced critical thinking skills.

It works with leading academics from the world's top universities to produce new analyses that focus on the ideas and the impact of the most influential works ever written across a wide variety of academic disciplines. Each of the works that sit at the heart of its growing library is an enduring example of great thinking. But by setting them in context – and looking at the influences that shaped their authors, as well as the responses they provoked – Macat encourages readers to look at these classics and game-changers with fresh eyes. Readers learn to think, engage and challenge their ideas, rather than simply accepting them.

'Macat offers an amazing first-of-its-kind tool for interdisciplinary learning and research. Its focus on works that transformed their disciplines and its rigorous approach, drawing on the world's leading experts and educational institutions, opens up a world-class education to anyone.'

Andreas Schleicher
Director for Education and Skills, Organisation for Economic Co-operation and Development

'Macat is taking on some of the major challenges in university education ... They have drawn together a strong team of active academics who are producing teaching materials that are novel in the breadth of their approach.'

Prof Lord Broers,
former Vice-Chancellor of the University of Cambridge

'The Macat vision is exceptionally exciting. It focuses upon new modes of learning which analyse and explain seminal texts which have profoundly influenced world thinking and so social and economic development. It promotes the kind of critical thinking which is essential for any society and economy. This is the learning of the future.'

Rt Hon Charles Clarke, former UK Secretary of State for Education

'The Macat analyses provide immediate access to the critical conversation surrounding the books that have shaped their respective discipline, which will make them an invaluable resource to all of those, students and teachers, working in the field.'

Professor William Tronzo, University of California at San Diego

WAYS IN TO THE TEXT

KEY POINTS

- Sheila Fitzpatrick, born in 1941, is an Australian historian of the Soviet Union,* a federation of European and Asian states that dissolved in 1991. Her focus is on the lives of ordinary people.

- *Everyday Stalinism* argues that Soviet* citizens made an enormous effort to continue to live "everyday lives," despite shortages, corruption, and fear of the regime.

- *Everyday Stalinism* was one of the first major post-Cold War* works of Soviet social history* that saw society as existing, in some small way, independently of the state.

Who Is Sheila Fitzpatrick?

Sheila Fitzpatrick, the author of *Everyday Stalinism: Ordinary Life in Extraordinary Times: Soviet Russia in the 1930s* (1999) is an Australian historian who specializes in the history of the Soviet Union. She currently teaches at the University of Sydney in Australia.

Fitzpatrick was born in 1941 and raised by socialist* parents. (For socialists, the tools and resources necessary for manufacturing and other types of business—"the means of production"—should be held in common hands.) She grew up during the first decades of the Cold War, a period of tension between two global powers marked by the threat of nuclear conflict.

On one side, the United States and its allies, including Australia, were democracies*—nations with elected leaders. Collectively known as "the West,"* their economies were, and continue to be, based on capitalism.* Under capitalism, trade and industry are conducted for private profit.

On the other side, the "Eastern Bloc" were countries allied with the Soviet Union (the Union of Soviet Socialist Republics, or USSR). Governed from the Russian capital of Moscow, the Soviet Union was a totalitarian* state, meaning the government had almost unlimited authority over the people, and that no challenge to the ruling Communist Party was allowed. Communism* is a form of socialism that attempts to abolish private property and social classes altogether.

Fitzpatrick's father, Brian Fitzpatrick,* was not an academic but an activist and revisionist* historian (someone who challenges widely accepted interpretations of history). He supported the 1917 overthrow of the Russian monarchy, known as the Russian Revolution,* but not the Soviet government that eventually followed. The left-wing perspective of Sheila's family led to her interest in and concern for ordinary people. When she became a historian she wrote the history of individuals such as peasants, workers, and intellectuals—an approach known as "history from below" or "social history"—rather than the history of monarchs, statesmen, and politicians. The historical importance of the Soviet Union when she was developing as a thinker clearly influenced her choice of research subject.

Fitzpatrick studied for her bachelor's degree at Melbourne University. She focused on the music and literature of the Soviet Union, an unusual approach at the time. Soviet studies routinely began with the uncomplicated premise that it was a brutal state—an adversary to be understood. It was not common to sympathize with its people. Fitzpatrick, however, was interested in the everyday life of the Soviet people, and spent much of her time reading Soviet journals and newspapers for information about its realities. She relocated to pursue a doctoral degree at the University of Oxford in the United Kingdom, where she continued her research on everyday life in the Soviet state.

What Does *Everyday Stalinism* Say?

Sheila Fitzpatrick's core question in this book is: How did normal Soviet citizens—*Homo Sovieticus** ("Soviet man") as she dubs them—deal with living in an overbearing state that tried to control everything? She was particularly interested in the 1930s, part of the period in which Joseph Stalin* was general secretary of the Communist Party and therefore, more importantly, the undisputed leader of the Soviet Union. Most Soviet citizens' everyday lives were all about dealing with shortages of consumer goods while trying to stay out of trouble with the state. Life was difficult; complaining or expressing opinions could be dangerous.

Everyday Stalinism, published in 1999, took a new approach to Soviet history. While recognizing the importance of the state, Fitzpatrick believed there was still such a thing as Soviet "society" that existed apart from the state, even if it was clearly affected by it. In this she is a revisionist historian, like her father. She acknowledged that the USSR used violence and oppression to control its population, but understood that it was still possible to live an everyday life despite the regime's demands and limitations. She aimed to integrate many of her fellow revisionists' broader arguments—about conformity, resistance, daily life—into a broader picture of the Soviet "everyday."

Fitzpatrick describes the Soviet Union as a "shortage economy"* because it was frequently difficult to purchase common consumer goods such as bread or toothpaste. It was a centrally planned economy in which the government decided how much of each consumer good should be produced, where it should be distributed and at what price. These decisions were imperfect, and shortages inevitably occurred. In a capitalist economy, competitive businesses motivated by profit eliminate most shortages quickly by producing more. The Soviet economy could not react nearly as quickly, so shortages led to corruption and hoarding. Despite the supposed elimination of social classes,* government officials and other elite citizens had greater access to goods, creating a patronage* system in which powerful people bought favors or loyalty with scarce consumer goods. Citizens competed for status through consumerism—merely owning a pair of stylish trousers, for example, indicated that a person had important connections. All of this gave rise to a black market*—a system in which goods are sold illegally. The black market became more important, Fitzpatrick argues, than the limited but officially permitted private sector of the 1920s.

Fitzpatrick offers three metaphors,* or symbolic descriptions, for the Soviet state's relations with its people:

- as a prison, focusing on the state's discipline of society
- as a boarding school, focusing on patriotism and respect for the state
- as a soup kitchen, focusing on the state as the provider of goods for the deserving poor.

Although the images of a prison and boarding school fit the totalitarian nature of the Soviet Union, Fitzpatrick thinks the most powerful metaphor is that of a soup kitchen, which positions the state both as a provider and a relief agency. Fitzpatrick's *Homo Sovieticus* (Soviet citizens) did not have to feel that they were part of a project of self-improvement, like students, or fear punishment, like prisoners. Neither did they have to feel gratitude for the soup kitchen; in fact, they may often have complained about not getting enough, or about favoritism toward other clients. Primarily, then, the Soviet citizen judged the kitchen based on the quantity and quality of goods it provided and how easy it was to obtain them.

Why Does *Everyday Stalinism* Matter?

Everyday Stalinism was widely praised for its research and accessibility, and has gone on to be the most important work of post-Cold War revisionist social history of Soviet everyday life. Fitzpatrick's penetration of the political sphere to look at the impact of economics and propaganda*—messages broadcast on state-owned media intended to mold society by shaping popular opinion—on everyday culture and social interactions has been recognized even by her critics, and testifies to its importance for the field.

Fitzpatrick broke the usual pattern of studying the Soviet Union as an abusive state in which society was a passive entity. Instead, she separates social relations from the state—that is, she attempts to look not at relations between individuals and the state but, rather, at interpersonal relations played out according to state-imposed rules and restrictions. The state was pervasive, but it did not control everything. Fitzpatrick's research was made possible by the opening of new government records in 1991, with the end of the Cold War. The Soviet Union broke into more than a dozen pieces, and Russia (by far the most powerful former Soviet state) became more open and liberal (that is, there was a greater degree of personal and economic liberty). As Russia became less of a threat to the West, it became less important to study the Soviet Union as a potential enemy of the US, or to focus on high-level decisionmaking, grand strategy, and the atrocities of the regime.

Some of Fitzpatrick's own students, themselves social historians and revisionists, studied many of the spheres of everyday life she covers in this book. Fitzpatrick has been influential in her methodology, insisting that students proceed from "empirical* novelty to the available theory rather than the other way around."[1] This means her followers begin their studies by observing data, and then move on to considering why it is the way it is. This is in contrast to the "theory first" approach, which begins with a theory and attempts to prove or disprove it with empirical evidence (evidence verifiable by observation).

While Fitzpatrick cannot be said to have *started* the debate as to whether or not there was a Soviet "society" independent of the state, she was prominent in leading the charge to "take the state out of" studies of society. Her work in the 1990s, of which *Everyday Stalinism* is the prime example, has reshaped Soviet historiography* (the techniques used for studying history).

Fitzpatrick's core idea is that in a time of revolutionary change, people's expectations and mindsets evolved dramatically as they searched for an ordinary, comfortable life. This has served as a starting point for both new investigations and criticisms.

NOTES

1   Jonathan Bone et al., "Roundtable: What Is a School? Is There a Fitzpatrick School of Soviet History?" *Acta Slavica Iaponica* 24 (2007): 233.

SECTION 1
INFLUENCES

MODULE 1
THE AUTHOR AND THE
HISTORICAL CONTEXT

KEY POINTS

- Sheila Fitzpatrick's *Everyday Stalinism* explores how ordinary people live under a totalitarian* state—a state defined by the intrusion of government into citizens' lives—amid economic scarcity, while still holding on to some sense of normality.

- Fitzpatrick's father headed a civil liberties* organization, which inspired his daughter to focus her studies on ordinary people.

- The end of the Cold War* between the United States and the Soviet Union* allowed Fitzpatrick access to archives, and to conduct her research without the problems associated with the earlier political context.

Why Read This Text?

Sheila Fitzpatrick's *Everyday Stalinism: Ordinary Life in Extraordinary Times: Soviet Russia in the 1930s* (1999) is an exploration of urban life in the Soviet Union of the 1930s, and of the emergence of *Homo Sovieticus** (a term that Fitzpatrick invented to refer to the everyday citizen under communism*—the political ideology of the Soviet Union). Her argument is that, following the relatively free 1920s, rapid industrialization* (in which an economy moves toward industrial production) and the imposition of Stalinist* cultural practices (defined by the aggressive political ideology of the nation's leader, Joseph Stalin),* the 1930s saw the creation of a new type of society dominated by economic scarcity, social changes, and pervasive surveillance* by the government.

> ❝ This book is an exploration of the everyday and the extraordinary in Stalin's Russia and how they interacted. It describes the ways in which Soviet citizens tried to live ordinary lives in the extraordinary circumstances of Stalinism. It presents a portrait of an emerging social species, *Homo Sovieticus*, for which Stalinism was the native habitat. ❞
>
> Sheila Fitzpatrick, *Everyday Stalinism: Ordinary Life in Extraordinary Times: Soviet Russia in the 1930s*

The text argues against looking at the Soviet Union simply as a totalitarian state that ruled through violence and threat. Fitzpatrick instead investigates the state's effect on the population and the ways in which citizens could operate within this state-imposed framework.

This is reflected in the title of the book, which stems from a wish to write about the "everyday life of ordinary people, 'little men' as opposed to the great."[1] The subtitle—*Ordinary Life in Extraordinary Times: Soviet Russia in the 1930s*—describes the struggle central to the book's research: the wish to live a normal life during a time of rapid and unprecedented political change. The struggle plays out during the creation of a new, Stalinist, social order.

Author's Life
Sheila Fitzpatrick is an Australian-born historian who currently teaches at the University of Sydney. She was educated at the universities of Melbourne, gaining her bachelor's degree in 1961, and Oxford, gaining her doctorate in 1969, and has written widely on aspects of modern Russian history, particularly the Soviet era. Her father headed a civil liberties organization,[2] which triggered her concern for ordinary people, and in part inspired her to write history "from below." In line with the aims of this kind of research and

analysis, she looks at the Soviet Union through the eyes of ordinary people—workers, peasants, or intellectuals, for example—rather than focusing primarily on the governing Communist* Party and the state.

Sheila Fitzpatrick's family and educational background affected her work in a variety of ways. She states that her father, Brian Fitzpatrick,* was a nonacademic radical historian and activist. He supported the Russian Revolution* of 1917, which led to the creation of the Soviet Union, but he was not necessarily a communist. This sparked his daughter's interest in Russian history, which she studied at Melbourne University; there, she concentrated on unusual themes—music and literature in the Soviet Union. This carried over to her graduate studies and subsequent career, in which she continues to use popular sources to gain insights into everyday life. She moved from Australia to the United Kingdom to study at Oxford, where she was disillusioned with the almost total lack of Sovietology* (study of the Soviet Union). Fitzpatrick states that she spent much of her time reading whatever Soviet journals and newspapers were available, showing again an early tendency to use popular media to glean information about what a Soviet citizen would have read and thought.[3]

Author's Background

Everyday Stalinism was published in 1999, at the end of a decade that had, in academic research terms, benefited greatly from the end of the Cold War and the fall of the USSR.* The opening of many Soviet government archives allowed historians to use previously inaccessible sources, moving beyond a reliance on the minutes of the Politburo* meetings (records of the meetings of high-level politicians) or other official party documents. The book is in many ways a product of the decade it was written in, building on previous ideas that could now be investigated properly due to the political changes of 1991.

Much of the decade's work aimed to use these new sources to answer questions about how people had lived under Soviet conditions, and to what extent the regime had succeeded in imposing its official ideology on people's private lives and thoughts. Fitzpatrick's work in many ways filled the need for a general work that tackled the concept of the "everyday" at a time when other historians were also turning to issues of Soviet society.

Joseph Stalin ruled between 1928 and 1953. However, the author does not give a chronological overview of his rise, and while political events that bear on society and culture are discussed, they are not the main object of investigation. Fitzpatrick also keeps in mind the study of totalitarian governments in general, drawing attention to universal spheres, such as the family, shopping, or the media, which can then be compared to other, non-Soviet regimes.

NOTES

1   Sheila Fitzpatrick, *Everyday Stalinism: Ordinary Life in Extraordinary Times: Soviet Russia in the 1930s* (New York: Oxford University Press, 1999), 1.

2   Johan Öberg, "Sheila Fitzpatrick: A Leading Lady in Soviet Studies," *Baltic Worlds* 1 (2012): 4–10.

3   Öberg, "Sheila Fitzpatrick," *Baltic Worlds* 1 (2012): 4–10.

MODULE 2
ACADEMIC CONTEXT

KEY POINTS

- Social history* is concerned, primarily, with history "from below," focusing especially on the disenfranchised and marginalized.

- Approaches to understanding the twentieth century in the Soviet Union* used either the "totalitarian model,"* which highlighted the exclusive role of the state in defining life, or "revisionist"* challenges to this orthodox interpretation, which questioned the role of governmental power.

- Revisionist historians such as the Lithuanian-born Moshe Lewin* and Stephen F. Cohen* of the United States were early influences on Fitzpatrick.

The Work in its Context

Sheila Fitzpatrick's *Everyday Stalinism: Ordinary Life in Extraordinary Times: Soviet Russia in the 1930s* is a work of social history, telling history "from below." Whereas, in the broadest sense, history "from above" is an effort to describe grand, dramatic events and the powerful participants in them, such as kings, dukes, diplomats, generals, and nations, "history from below" is the study of the everyday, usual, and under-recorded. It focuses on women, peasants, merchants, and disenfranchised people who make up a nation, but whose individual stories are not considered significant.

"History from below" was a phrase coined by the French historian Lucien Febvre* of the *Annales* School*—an approach to history that emphasized the study of "total history." This meant looking at the "everyday" in addition to dramatic events, and at factors such as geography and economic development.

> ❝ 'We have created a new type of state!' Lenin
> repeatedly claimed. He made it clear at the same
> time that he considered this new state to be radically
> different from a constitutional democracy with its civil
> liberties. ❞
>
> Carl Friedrich and Zbigniew Brzezinski, *Totalitarian Dictatorship and Autocracy*

The German social historian Jürgen Kocka,* in his *Industrial Culture*, a history of modernization in Germany, wrote that social history "gave priority to the study of particular kinds of phenomena, such as classes and movements, urbanization and industrialization,* family and education, work and leisure, mobility, inequality, conflicts and revolutions." Social history tends to employ the analytical techniques of the social sciences* (fields such as economics, political science, and sociology—the study of social behavior) rather than merely attempting to relate a sequence of major events.[1]

Overview of the Field

There were two major approaches to Russian history in the twentieth century: the totalitarian and the revisionist.

A major proponent of the totalitarian model was the American political scientist Zbigniew Brzezinski,* who served as national security advisor to US President Jimmy Carter.* He and others, among them the German American political theorist Carl Friedrich,* identified different aspects of totalitarian regimes, such as a guiding ideology, control of the media and communications, state planning in the economy, and widespread terror. Research guided by this model painted the USSR* (the Union of Soviet Socialist Republics) as a uniquely evil regime, and focused on the highest tier of Soviet* politics—the policymaking committee known as the Politburo,* the ruling Communist Party, and planners. The revisionist historians challenged this approach, focusing instead on the bureaucrats* who carried out these plans and on society in general, including women, peasants, and workers.

Brzezinski and Friedrich believed totalitarianism* was "the regime's efforts to remold and transform the human beings under its control in the image of its ideology," meaning the regime was in "total control of the everyday life of its citizens."[2] So, if the regime is infinitely powerful, and exercises an unlimited degree of control over its citizens, then the "everyday" simply becomes an extension of the "political." By this logic, it makes little sense to study the "everyday" as anything other than another expression of the political.

Revisionist approaches, on the other hand, aim instead to uncover a more complex society. "Revisionists," Fitzpatrick argues, "many of whom were or aspired to be social historians, depicted the Soviet Union in bottom-up rather than top-down terms," and tried to figure out where and why social support for the regime might have occurred. They reasoned that there must have been people beyond the top leaders who had benefited from the regime.[3] In a 1986 article, Fitzpatrick wrote, "The 'totalitarian' view of Stalinist rule correctly emphasizes the regime's transformationalist aspirations in explaining coercion and terror," meaning that traditional Sovietology* (study of the Soviet Union) was correct in assuming that Stalin's* regime aimed to remake every element of society through the use of force. However, "the actual control exercised by the Stalinist regime was often limited, as social historians looking from the bottom up have begun to point out."[4]

Academic Influences

Fitzpatrick's work followed on from that of earlier revisionists, such as Roy Medvedev* of Russia, Moshe Lewin, and Stephen F. Cohen of the US.[5] One of the key elements of revisionism was to reject the idea that Stalinism,* terror, and totalitarianism were essential features of Soviet life. For example, as Lewin writes in his 1968 book *Lenin's Last Struggle*, Vladimir Lenin,* the architect of the Russian Revolution* of 1917 and of the early Soviet state that immediately followed, recommended a less totalitarian (but still utopian,* or idealistic) vision. Lenin suggested, among other things, that the new state should be committed to "(1) abandoning the unrealistic socialist vision and aiming instead at 'state capitalism' and the market economy the country so badly needed, (2) making, so to speak, a political pact with the peasantry: promoting development of a free, rural cooperative movement and refraining … from any compulsion." He also suggested allowing (or even encouraging) dissent within the party.[6] The revisionists saw Stalin not as the inheritor of Lenin's dream, but as its corruptor.

Cohen argued that it was an oversimplification to assume that a small group had always aimed for totalitarian control over a passive body of citizens. This notion served a political purpose, because a great deal of Sovietology was taking place in the US, which was engaged in the long period of tension marked by the threat of nuclear conflict known as the Cold War* with the USSR. "But the politicization of an academic field does have serious intellectual consequences," Cohen said. Scholarship that is somehow linked to policy tends to accept traditional views, and to make simplified interpretations of complicated facts for the purpose of making predictions.[7]

NOTES

1 Jürgen Kocka, *Industrial Culture and Bourgeois Society: Business, Labor, and Bureaucracy in Modern Germany* (New York: Berghahn Books, 1999), 276.

2 Carl J. Friedrich and Zbigniew Brzezinski, *Totalitarian Dictatorship and Autocracy* (New York: Frederick A. Praeger, 1968), 10.

3   Sheila Fitzpatrick, "Revisionism in Soviet History," *History and Theory* 46, no. 4 (2007): 81.

4   Sheila Fitzpatrick, "New Perspectives on Stalinism," *The Russian Review* 45, no. 4 (1986): 366.

5   Fitzpatrick, "Revisionism in Soviet History," 82.

6   Moshe Lewin, *Lenin's Last Struggle,* trans. A. M. Sheridan Smith (Ann Arbor: University of Michigan Press, 2005), xxix.

7   Stephen F. Cohen, *Rethinking the Soviet Experience: Politics and History Since 1917* (Oxford: Oxford University Press, 1985), 12.

MODULE 3
THE PROBLEM

KEY POINTS

- Fitzpatrick's question was: How did Soviet* citizens survive and advance themselves despite the powerful Stalinist* state (the aggressively intrusive government run according to the political ideology and policies of Joseph Stalin)?*

- Other scholars tended to focus on specific aspects of everyday life under Stalinism, analyzing either the realms of public life, private life, or conformity.

- *Everyday Stalinism* encompasses all these research areas, and Fitzpatrick draws them together to present a complex Soviet citizen rather than the helpless peasant of the "totalitarian model."*

Core Question

In *Everyday Stalinism: Ordinary Life in Extraordinary Times: Soviet Russia in the 1930s*, Sheila Fitzpatrick's core question asks how Soviet citizens—*Homo Sovieticus*,* in her words—dealt with the practices and institutions that made up Stalinism. The lives of most citizens were filled with constant concerns about survival and advancement. The regime had an impact on nearly everything—shopping for food or clothes, interacting with family, getting ahead in work and life, reading newspapers, or expressing opinions.

Everyday Stalinism stands alongside other books of the mid- to late 1990s and early 2000s in terms of the sources on which its analysis was based, and the theoretical approach that informed this analysis. Prior to the fall of the USSR* in 1991, much study of Soviet society was undertaken according to the highly politicized "totalitarian model," which assumed that an all-powerful Soviet state controlled every

> ❝ Few histories of everyday life start with a chapter on government and bureaucracy. But it is one of the peculiarities of our subject that the state can never be kept out, try though we may. Soviet citizens attempting to live ordinary lives were continually running up against the state in one of its multifarious aspects. ❞
>
> Sheila Fitzpatrick, *Everyday Stalinism: Ordinary Life in Extraordinary Times: Soviet Russia in the 1930s*

element of everyday life through terror. This reflected an understanding of the Soviet Union as an "evil empire," in contrast to the open societies of the West.*

Fitzpatrick extensively cites a new generation of post-Soviet scholars, and her earlier work in social history* can be seen as having been an inspiration for them. Some scholars sought to use newly accessible archives to go over old debates. These included the reasons for the Great Purge* of the 1930s (the name given to the period in which Stalin killed or imprisoned many members of the Communist Party), or the true numbers of the dead after the forced collectivization,* when individual farms and workers were made to form collective farms. But Fitzpatrick is more interested in studying the impact of official ideology on people and their self-identity (roughly, the way they understand themselves), and on the experience of living under a totalitarian* regime.

The Participants

Fitzpatrick's work relates to a number of other revisionist* scholars working on Soviet social history, all of whom challenged the orthodoxy by seeking alternatives to the totalitarian model, including Sarah Davies* of the United Kingdom, Russian American Elena Osokina,* and the American academics Stephen Kotkin* and Jochen Hellbeck.*

Kotkin's work is of particular importance to Fitzpatrick, especially his book *Magnetic Mountain*.[1] The book focuses on the relationship between the state and workers in a single industrial city, Magnitogorsk,* which became central to Stalin's drive toward industrialization* (a nationwide increase in industrial production). Kotkin's core idea was that citizens learned to conform outwardly to official expectations in order to get ahead. He called this "speaking Bolshevik,"* referring to the original name for what became the Communist Party. Kotkin's work differs from Fitzpatrick's in that he is heavily concerned with the domination of life by work. Fitzpatrick leaves the workplace out of her own research, showing that Soviet man actually "speaks Bolshevik" in all areas of life. She also takes a more materialistic viewpoint, arguing that shortages were more important than ideological conformity in shaping Soviet identity ("materialist" here signifying the importance of economic and physical factors).

Scholars such as the historians Sarah Davies and Jochen Hellbeck, meanwhile, have shown how, even in the darkest times of repression, Soviet citizens could express their own opinions. Davies investigated popular opinion when Stalinist repression was at its toughest—during the Great Purge—and showed how letter-writing and complaints became a way for citizens to criticize shortages, social policies, and even the heroic image of Stalin and other top leaders as portrayed by state propaganda.*[2]

Hellbeck uses diaries to show how certain citizens saw the advantages in "becoming cultured" and rising in the ranks, and shaped their image and identity according to official expectations. Both authors are extremely illuminating, and have greatly influenced Fitzpatrick. She pays attention to the relationship between citizens' complaints and the regime, as well as to some activists' interest in becoming model communists. She combines all these things—the very private (diaries), the public (complaints), and the conformist ("speaking Bolshevik")— into an argument that applies to all Soviet urban experiences.[3]

The Contemporary Debate

In order to understand Fitzpatrick's argument, it is important to understand what she and her fellow revisionist historians aim to achieve. The totalitarian model for studying the Soviet Union leaves no place for individual free will, seeing people as oppressed and voiceless. Revisionist historians, while accepting that the USSR used violence and powerful oppression to control its population, seek to understand how the masses lived and acted when faced with the regime's demands and limitations. Whereas her fellow revisionists focused on how people resisted in particular situations, Fitzpatrick aims to integrate many of their arguments—conformity, resistance, daily life—into a broader picture of the Soviet "everyday."

Fitzpatrick describes how the regime gained compliance from its population partly through a patronage* system, in which valuable goods were provided to certain citizens in return for loyalty or favors. As the Soviet state ran the economy, allocation of goods became a major function of the bureaucracy* (the various offices and departments of state administration), and access to goods became a status symbol and a source of power.[4] So getting ahead in the Soviet Union meant making friends in the right places, or using your own position to benefit others. Patronage was, then, yet another tool by which the state could control its population, by tying people to it in unofficial ways.

NOTES

1 Stephen Kotkin, *Magnetic Mountain: Stalinism as Civilization* (Berkeley: University of California Press, 1997).

2 Sarah Davies, *Popular Opinion in Stalin's Russia: Terror, Propaganda, and Dissent 1934–1941* (Cambridge: Cambridge University Press, 1997).

3 Jochen Hellbeck, *Revolution on My Mind: Writing a Diary Under Stalin* (Cambridge: Harvard University Press, 2006).

4 Sheila Fitzpatrick, *Everyday Stalinism: Ordinary Life in Extraordinary Times: Soviet Russia in the 1930s* (New York: Oxford University Press, 1999), 114.

MODULE 4
THE AUTHOR'S CONTRIBUTION

KEY POINTS

- *Everyday Stalinism* aims to show what "normal" life under Stalin's* Russia* looked like, and how people live a "normal" life in extraordinary circumstances.

- Fitzpatrick uses sources from the state (such as official propaganda)* along with sources from everyday life (such as diaries) to show how the state created the circumstances in which everyday life occurred.

- Fitzpatrick does not consider social class* or the workplace in describing everyday life; these omissions place limitations on her work.

Author's Aims

Sheila Fitzpatrick's *Everyday Stalinism: Ordinary Life in Extraordinary Times: Soviet Russia in the 1930s* describes how citizens struggled to lead a "normal" life during the "extraordinary" circumstances of Stalinism,* with its revolutionary plans, economic changes, and widespread state interference in private lives. In her own words, the book "presents a portrait of an emerging social species, *Homo Sovieticus,** for which Stalinism was the native habitat."[1] It focuses on everyday practices, as well as on the strategies people develop to survive and advance in an oppressive society.

Fitzpatrick does not aim to illustrate any particular theory about everyday life, but instead to describe the "extraordinary everydayness" of Soviet* times,[2] and to look at the state's plan for realizing a particular type of socialism.* She investigates the methods used by the state— such as industrialization* and surveillance* (observation by

> ❝ People understand and remember their lives in terms of stories. These stories make sense out of the scattered data of ordinary life, providing a context, imposing a pattern that shows where one has come from and where one is going. ❞
>
> Sheila Fitzpatrick, *Everyday Stalinism: Ordinary Life in Extraordinary Times: Soviet Russia in the 1930s*

authority)—to create a system that people had to navigate, and the tactics they needed to use to do so. Citizens became rivals as they competed for scarce everyday products, which led them to distrust each other. The fact that all goods came from the state gave citizens a reason to seek the state's favor by informing on fellow citizens. Toward the end of the book, Fitzpatrick explores how this behavior became a tool for the Great Purge* of the 1930s (also called the Great Terror), in which hundreds of thousands of Communist Party members and others were executed as Stalin sought to entrench his power.

Approach

Fitzpatrick brings together the study of key aspects of everyday life, such as housing, family problems, and food and clothes shortages, to give a wide picture of the many aspects of a person's life. Her approach is also driven by her sources, as she shows how everyday dealings between state and citizen were perceived on both sides of the interaction. In addition to state documents and propaganda, she relies on interviews and oral history, letters to the regime and popular culture. So she takes a dual approach, asking: What did the state intend and what conditions, both cultural and economic, did it create? And how did personal relationships develop and change under these new circumstances?

She deliberately leaves out discussion of the workplace, arguing that focusing on specific professions would get in the way of talking about a unified experience, while the field of "citizenry" and urban life allows her to do just that. This is a problem, because work was a major part of the "everyday" experience; it was central to Stalinist propaganda—building Soviet socialism meant grand feats of labor. Fitzpatrick's decision to dismiss class relationships as unimportant to 1930s society is also problematic. Like labor, social class took a central place in communist* communications, and appeared in court cases, administrative practices, and even language. Ignoring this factor makes it hard for the reader to understand a society that was saturated in the language of class.

Fitzpatrick concludes by discussing her three metaphors,* or symbols, for the relationship between the Soviet state and citizen. These painted the state as:
- a prison, focusing on the discipline of society
- a boarding school, focusing on patriotism and respect for the state
- a soup kitchen, providing goods for the deserving poor.

Each of these metaphors portray the state as paternalistic*— controlling and disciplining individuals because they cannot be trusted to run their own lives. These images play an important role in the types of behaviors Fitzpatrick describes among the populace.

Contribution in Context

While Fitzpatrick is very conscious of the work of other historians, she does not fully accept their ideas; she modifies their conclusions by looking beyond the narrow field that they tended to investigate. This is partly thanks to her own long experience, as the works cited are the first books of young scholars, who had not been working in the area for as long as Fitzpatrick. Her experience allowed her to blend their arguments, already influenced by her revisionist* approach of the 1970s and 1980s, into a deep analysis of what it meant to be a Soviet citizen in the 1930s.

She is also aware of Russian historiography* (techniques for studying history), and she serves as a bridge between the then-untranslated work of the Russian scholar Elena Osokina* and Western scholarship. Osokina's work investigated the consumption patterns of Soviet citizens, which are central to Fitzpatrick's argument.[3] Other Soviet scholarship of the 1990s also interests her. She extensively cites Stephen Kotkin's *Magnetic Mountain*, for example,[4] which in its investigation of state-society interaction*—the relationship between the people and the state and its institutions—is similar to that of Fitzpatrick in both the sources used (focusing on citizens), and in its argument that the field on which social interactions play out is created by the state's various projects.

NOTES

1 Sheila Fitzpatrick, *Everyday Stalinism: Ordinary Life in Extraordinary Times: Soviet Russia in the 1930s* (New York: Oxford University Press, 1999), 1.

2 Fitzpatrick, *Everyday Stalinism*, 2.

3 Elena Osokina, *Hierarchy of Consumption: Life Under the Stalinist Rationing System 1928–1935* (Moscow: MGOU, 1993).

4 Stephen Kotkin, *Magnetic Mountain: Stalinism as Civilization* (Berkeley: University of California Press, 1997).

SECTION 2
IDEAS

MODULE 5
MAIN IDEAS

KEY POINTS

- The key themes of *Everyday Stalinism* are the shortages of consumer goods that defined the Soviet* economy and the pervasive nature of the state.

- *Homo Sovieticus** ("Soviet man") is both dependent on the state and critical of it, obsessed with consumption in a shortage economy,* and ultimately able to live a normal life by navigating the state's confusing and secretive institutions.

- Fitzpatrick's reliance on storytelling works two ways: it makes the work easier to read, but it was criticized for being potentially biased.

Key Themes

Sheila Fitzpatrick's argument in *Everyday Stalinism: Ordinary Life in Extraordinary Times: Soviet Russia in the 1930s* rests on two themes: the shortage economy (the chronic shortages of consumer goods experienced by those living in a centrally planned economy) and the inescapabilty of the Soviet state. Both stem from the regime's vision of society: a socialist* utopia* (an ideal world of equality and common ownership of businesses, trade, and production), which was to be administered by the enlightened Bolshevik* elite (high-ranking members of the Communist* Party), using the one-party state* to replace previously free associations in all spheres of life. So, Fitzpatrick argues, every action a citizen could take was connected with the state in some way. At the same time, this state was promoting an image of abundance and a bright future that would overcome the "backwardness" of the old Russia.[1] This created a language that

> **"** Even if shortages could be rationalized, however, they could not be disregarded. They were already a central fact of economic and everyday life. **"**
>
> Sheila Fitzpatrick, *Everyday Stalinism: Ordinary Life in Extraordinary Times: Soviet Russia in the 1930s*

citizens could use to express their hopes and requests, and a set of standards to evaluate the state and sometimes to complain about it.

Combined, the argument therefore ties together the shortages and official propaganda* with the realities of everyday life to illustrate Soviet citizens' actions and thoughts. The exploration of *Homo Sovieticus* has proven useful to other scholars as a novel approach to discussing the people who fall between the extremes of buying into or completely rejecting the ideals of a totalitarian* state. Fitzpatrick restores choice to her subjects, complicating the picture and reminding her readers that history is made up of millions of citizens, rather than just state institutions and government decisions.

Exploring the Ideas

The shortage economy is one of Fitzpatrick's central preoccupations. The shortages led to inequality, in which some people had access to restaurants and goods from closed shops, while most could obtain necessities only through speculation and *blat** (a Russian term meaning favors and patronage).* This gave rise to the black market,* a second economy in which goods were traded illegally. Fitzpatrick argues that the black market became even more important to people's lives than the limited but officially permitted private sector in the 1920s.[2]

Fitzpatrick compares this difficult reality to the "images of abundance" that the regime promoted, promising that socialism would bring plenty to all.[3] Soviet people became obsessed with goods as status symbols, and consumption became a dividing factor in a society that was supposed to be building classless socialism. The differences between socialist and capitalist* consumption were striking: Soviet advertising described the consumption of certain domestic goods (such as personal hygiene products) as a marker of culture and civilization. Fitzpatrick contrasts this official image with the realities of the black market, via which goods acquired importance through scarcity, rather than civilizational usefulness.

A theme running throughout the book is the influence of the Soviet state. Fitzpatrick offers three metaphors,* or symbolic models, for the Soviet state's relations with people. The state is described as:

- a prison
- a boarding school
- a soup kitchen.

She settles on the last as the best description of the Stalinist* USSR.* While the comparisons with a prison and boarding school capture the discipline and control that the state employed, they are too close to the totalitarian model of society. Instead, the image of a soup kitchen describes the state as both provider and relief agency. Customers (the Soviet citizens) did not have to make an effort to improve themselves (like a student), or live in fear of punishment (like a prisoner); nor did they need to feel grateful for the soup kitchen. They could even criticize the kitchen for giving too little or playing favorites with the other clients. The citizen's judgment of the kitchen was solely based on the quantity and goods it provided, and how easy it was to obtain them.[4]

So, the Soviet citizen that Fitzpatrick aims to describe is someone dependent on the state, but who nevertheless criticizes it. Accordingly, she casts doubt on the success of the utopian propaganda peddled by the state, and on the amount of fear that people felt. Her main idea rests on this metaphor. Soviet citizens became adept at navigating the state's rules and shortcomings, often forming personal ties to get ahead. Soviets conformed publicly but aimed to improve their standing and living standards privately. Much like the soup kitchen client, Soviet individuals were thus "survivors"—which is how Fitzpatrick concludes her argument and her book.[5]

Language and Expression

Fitzpatrick published *Everyday Stalinism* in 1999, recently enough for her text to pose few problems for the modern reader in terms of language. Although the book's reliance on storytelling makes it easier to read, this has also led to criticism. Roberta Manning,* a historian at Boston College who reviewed the book for a scholarly journal, argues that Fitzpatrick is more concerned with illustrating her wider points than with examining the evidence critically.

Manning also levels a more serious criticism at Fitzpatrick's use of the Harvard Project of Oral History,* a resource containing, among other recorded narratives concerning totalitarian states, stories told about the Soviet Union by Soviet refugees. According to the reviewer, the respondents' views drive Fitzpatrick's conclusion that the typical Soviet citizen was both passive and a risk-taker. Manning says she fails to consider that the interviewees were often not typical Soviet citizens but political refugees selected by a politicized organization opposed to the USSR (called "Vlasovite," named for Andrey Vlasov,* a Soviet general who changed sides during World War II). For Manning, Fitzpatrick's conclusions may rest on biased evidence.[6]

While it is easy to see why Fitzpatrick uses people's stories to illustrate her society-wide argument, her reliance on the Harvard Project is harder to explain, given the participants. This problem is lessened by the fact that she uses a variety of other popular sources to support her conclusions, so the view of the Soviet citizen as passive is not derived from the Harvard Project alone.

NOTES

1   Sheila Fitzpatrick, *Everyday Stalinism: Ordinary Life in Extraordinary Times: Soviet Russia in the 1930s* (New York: Oxford University Press, 1999), 15.

2   Fitzpatrick, *Everyday Stalinism*, 66.

3   Fitzpatrick, *Everyday Stalinism,* 90.

4   Fitzpatrick, *Everyday Stalinism,* 226–7.

5   Fitzpatrick, *Everyday Stalinism,* 227.

6   Roberta T. Manning, "Review of *Everyday Stalinism,*" *American Historical Review* 105, no. 5 (2000): 1839.

MODULE 6
SECONDARY IDEAS

KEY POINTS

- Within the framework of the larger argument about everyday life, scarcity, and the Soviet" state, Fitzpatrick discusses a number of specific elements of life: family, social mobility, and repression.
- Despite the supposed elimination of social classes* under Stalinism,* the wives of factory workers played more of a leadership role in their families than the wives of high-ranking government officials.
- Patronage* (the system of providing goods in exchange for favors or loyalty) violated the principles of central planning, yet was also made necessary by central planning.

Other Ideas

While the main claims of *Everyday Stalinism: Ordinary Life in Extraordinary Times: Soviet Russia in the 1930s* rest on Sheila Fitzpatrick's arguments about the shortage economy,* the pervasiveness of the state, and the impact these had on the creation of the Soviet citizen (*Homo Sovieticus*),* her investigation of a wide range of everyday practices reveals many secondary arguments about different aspects of Soviet life.

These secondary areas include family, social mobility, repression, and propaganda.* They are interesting to the reader in their own right, as they touch on many parts of everyday life that do not fit exclusively within Fitzpatrick's main point about the shortage economy and the state. For example, she clearly shows how families were subject to the same forces that shaped identity elsewhere—the need to provide for children, or to deal with an absent provider (in this case the husband and not just the state).

f It is about what it meant to be privileged in
Stalinist society, as well as what it meant to be one of
the millions of social outcasts. It is about the police
surveillance that was endemic to this society, and
the epidemics of terror like the Great Purges that
periodically cast it into turmoil. For *Homo Sovieticus*, the
state was a central and ubiquitous presence. ™

Sheila Fitzpatrick, *Everyday Stalinism: Ordinary Life in Extraordinary Times:
Soviet Russia in the 1930s*

Fitzpatrick's focus on the family and on women builds on a new
interest in Soviet gender politics by scholars such as Wendy Goldman,*
a professor at Carnegie Mellon University. This and other secondary
topics reflect the availability of new sources that have opened up more
spheres of Soviet life to research; these provide inspiration for further
studies of the family, popular culture, and the experience of the groups
considered outcasts in Soviet society.

Exploring the Ideas

Fitzpatrick describes how state propaganda of the 1930s focused on
how society could become more civilized by purchasing certain
products, such as personal hygiene goods. This may not have increased
product sales, but the general emphasis on "becoming cultured" and
modern, in terms of departing from traditional life and values, was
widely accepted. Soviet citizens had wider access than in earlier years
to state-sanctioned literature, movies, and news media. The state
created an image of a well-rounded person who should know about
Shakespeare's* plays, African geography, and German poetry, as well as
famous engineers and feats of Soviet technology.[1] This emphasis on
culture was part of a wide-reaching sense of upward social mobility
that Soviet citizens were experiencing during this period. Fitzpatrick

argues that there was a feeling, among young people especially, that the Soviet regime was giving them the chance to rise, but not at the expense of anyone else. Instead, they were to do it together with "the people," who were also being uplifted by economic changes and cultural programs.

Fitzpatrick also explores the changes to family life that Stalinism brought about. She delineates the division between women in high-ranking positions or the wives of powerful members of the Communist Party, and those who worked in factories and were married to ordinary workers. Fitzpatrick argues that for higher-placed women, the priorities were duty to their husbands, homemaking, and presenting a cultured and loyal image. For ordinary women, however, the husband was often incapable of carrying out family duties (due to working hours or drink), meaning women's responsibility was to the family in general. They took the brunt of the shortage economy, trying to clothe and feed the family, often in the absence of a husband, while also seeing some of their previous rights eroded (such as the right to abortion). Fitzpatrick argues that due to family problems, ordinary women therefore became especially adept at navigating the Soviet network of consumption, and had very different experiences from those of women higher up.[2]

While she did not set out to explain the Great Terror* of 1937–8 (when many hundreds of thousands of people were executed in the name of ideological purity, as Joseph Stalin* sought to entrench his power) or the repressive mechanisms of the regime, Fitzpatrick does dedicate a number of chapters to these topics. She examines how people and groups who were "socially alien" became outcasts, such as the old bourgeois* (the wealthy upper-middle class who owned property and businesses), and how this encouraged people to conceal their identities and make up life stories. Some actually accepted the regime's criticisms, coming to feel truly inferior, while others tried to gain acceptance through exaggerated loyalty.[3] This constant creation of enemies, and of an anxious Soviet patriotism that sought to exclude "undesirables," fed into the eventual mass denunciations* of the late 1930s.

Overlooked

Fitzpatrick raises a number of points that have largely been overlooked by scholars. In her conclusion, she states that the obstacles a citizen faced, and the uncertain personal relations he or she had to build in order to get ahead, resulted in the belief that luck played a major part in anyone's success or failure. Indeed, "risk-taking was sometimes a necessity for effective functioning."[4] For bureaucrats* (those working in administrative positions) it could be worth risking imprisonment in order to rise to the top, while citizens could play the dangerous game of denouncing those same bosses.

Patronage meant that people had to take risks through illegal transactions and favors, and this went both for the patron and the client. Fitzpatrick points out that this seemingly irrational and gambling mentality was the "direct antithesis [opposite] of the rational planning mentality" that the regime undertook in its five-year plans.[5] These plans were a series of five-year, nationwide economic and production targets, which then formed the basis for business decisions rather than market forces. Regularity and predictability were the slogans of this type of thinking; choice and initiative were unacceptable. Patronage had no place in the rational order of Soviet planning, and yet it was precisely this planning that created the patronage system. Planned distribution meant shortages; planning meant a bureaucracy that had access to goods and services it could trade with clients on a personal basis.

This has, as yet, been overlooked by studies. This is partly due to insufficient understanding of interactions between state and society in Soviet studies in particular, and in totalitarian* studies in general. Although risk seems to have played an important role in the makeup of Fitzpatrick's *Homo Sovieticus,* it still awaits its examination in studies of the Soviet Union.

NOTES

1   Sheila Fitzpatrick, *Everyday Stalinism: Ordinary Life in Extraordinary Times: Soviet Russia in the 1930s* (New York: Oxford University Press, 1999), 88.

2   Fitzpatrick, *Everyday Stalinism,* 162.

3   Fitzpatrick, *Everyday Stalinism,* 138.

4   Fitzpatrick, *Everyday Stalinism*, 221.

5   Fitzpatrick, *Everyday Stalinism,* 221.

MODULE 7
ACHIEVEMENT

KEY POINTS

- While, for Fitzpatrick, the state exerted a massive influence, her book also focuses on interpersonal relationships; this is not a contradiction but an acknowledgement of the overwhelming power of the state to affect the everyday.

- Totalitarianism* was not limited to the Soviet Union;* totalitarian states still exist around the world, contributing to the continued popularity of Fitzpatrick's book.

- Fitzpatrick was criticized for her sole focus on Russia:* the urban makeup of Soviet Ukraine,* for example, a separate part of the Soviet Union, was different from that of Russia.

Assessing the Argument

As a study of the "everyday," Sheila Fitzpatrick's *Everyday Stalinism: Ordinary Life in Extraordinary Times: Soviet Russia in the 1930s* focuses on the private lives of individuals. Fitzpatrick takes up her own challenge in trying not to see all social relations as fundamentally involving the state, and in attempting instead to look at interpersonal relations played out according to state-imposed rules and restrictions. While the pervasiveness of a state that aimed to transform society on every level through control and planning cannot be forgotten, the reader should not mistake this for a contradiction on her part. It is impossible to talk about Soviet history without considering the regime's aims, as it used the one-party state* to mold the economy, culture, and even personal beliefs.

Indeed, Fitzpatrick argues that everyday interactions in the Soviet Union inevitably involved the state in some way—even if she finds it

> ❝ The pervasiveness of the state in urban Russia
> of the 1930s has led me to define the "everyday"
> for the purposes of this book in terms of everyday
> interactions that in some way involved the state ... But
> the definition can scarcely be seen as narrow, since
> it includes such diverse topics as shopping, traveling,
> celebrating, telling jokes, finding an apartment, getting
> an education, securing a job, advancing in one's career,
> cultivating patrons and connections, marrying and
> rearing children, writing complaints and denunciations,
> voting, and trying to steer clear of the secret police. ❞
>
> Sheila Fitzpatrick, *Everyday Stalinism: Ordinary Life in Extraordinary Times:
> Soviet Russia in the 1930s*

far more interesting to see how people used the regime's language and
limitations to navigate their everyday surroundings. It is where the
everyday social need for necessities ran up against the state's
revolutionary and rapid industrialization* drive that she draws the
clearest contrast between the "everyday" and the "extraordinary" in
the USSR of the 1930s.

Fitzpatrick explores the Soviet effort to remake society from what
it considered a backward mass of peasants into a modern, urban, and
industrial community that could build socialism.* In doing so, it used
a language of utopianism* to justify an economic focus on heavy
industry, arguing that if everyone abandoned their previous way of life
and contributed to industrialization,* the Soviet Union could
become a utopia—a paradise. People and resources were shifted to
heavy industry on a vast scale, creating constant shortages of food and
consumer goods. In this way, interpersonal relations and everyday
matters such as shopping or family life were affected by the state's
plans, even if they didn't directly involve the bureaucracy* in a

particular citizen's case. This is a critical point: readers should not interpret every instance of the state's interference as proof that the state ran every aspect of life. Instead, the state should be seen as the provider of the goods and rules than ran everyday life, in a sense creating the "playing field" where Soviet citizens worked, lived, and thought.

Achievement in Context

The subject of the book—everyday life in a totalitarian socialist state—is applicable to other times and places too, including other revolutionary periods, such as China's Great Leap Forward* (an attempt, from 1958, to forcibly transform China from an agricultural to an industrial country; it led to millions of deaths from famine and state violence). The scale of transformation and the methods described in *Everyday Stalinism* are particular to the communist* system of the time, but do not prevent the text from being useful for other topics. The Soviet state continued to promote a socialist future and sought to control everyday interactions and the economy almost until its collapse in 1991; similar systems were set up in Eastern Europe, China, Vietnam, Cuba, and many other communist states after World War II.*

Fitzpatrick's interest in identities, and the formation of identities, is applicable not just to states that used the same political model but also to other totalitarian and even nontotalitarian regimes. Nazi Germany* and Fascist Italy* both aimed to transform their societies and people through similar campaigns that relied on the paternalistic* state, so the ideas discussed in *Everyday Stalinism* can be used as a theoretical tool to approach them too.

Limitations

Fitzpatrick's focus only on the Russian part of the Soviet Union has exposed her to some criticism, such as that by Serhy Yekelchuk,* a Ukrainian professor. He notes that while processes similar to those Fitzpatrick identifies in Russia were occurring in Soviet Ukraine* too, there were differences due to the urban makeup of cities. This point makes Fitzpatrick's analysis seem somewhat limited.

This criticism can be generalized, in that even though various states may use similar techniques to shape and mobilize their societies, the cultural and historical specifics of each society may differ. Historical developments in China or Cuba would not produce exactly the same type of interaction between society and state as in Soviet Russia. For example, a patronage* network (or *blat** as it was called in Russian) may differ widely depending on the particular social structures being modified by the intrusive state.

However, this criticism still recognizes that there is much merit in Fitzpatrick's analysis, as everyday life is changed significantly in any intrusive, controlling state. Moreover, Fitzpatrick concerns herself with truly universal topics such as the family or shopping, which concern the state in any regime. Even democratic* regimes (societies in which elections are held for leaders) have an impact on everyday life through laws about child support, for example, or subsidies to families and businesses. The "everyday" is one of the most global experiences, and Fitzpatrick's analysis has revealed just how much more room there is for exploration of the topic.

MODULE 8
PLACE IN THE AUTHOR'S WORK

KEY POINTS

- *Everyday Stalinism* is Fitzpatrick's most important work. It serves to consolidate her previous work, which investigated the life and values of Soviet* society, as opposed to seeing society merely as a product of government.

- Fitzpatrick's entire body of work is highly integrated, and consistently defends the viewpoint that while the state profoundly affected Soviet society, society itself had influence that went beyond the power of the state.

- A challenge to dominant historical narratives, *Everyday Stalinism* is an important work of revisionist* history, and inspired others to "open up" the totalitarian* state.

Positioning

Sheila Fitzpatrick's *Everyday Stalinism: Ordinary Life in Extraordinary Times: Soviet Russia in the 1930s,* published in 1999, is the work of a mature author who had already written extensively on different aspects of Soviet society and culture. It reflects many of the concerns of her earlier career, and expands on a number of the cultural themes that she investigated from her very first book, *The Commissariat of Enlightenment: Soviet Organization of Education and the Arts under Lunacharsky* (1970). The Commissariat of Enlightenment,* headed by Anatoly Lunacharsky,* was founded immediately after the Russian Revolution* to enlighten the citizens through education and the arts.[1] Fitzpatrick's book charted the rise of the commissariat's bureaucracy* and its attempts to spread a certain philosophy among the population, and the effects this had on social mobility in the USSR.*

> **❝** Collectivization was a traumatic experience for Russian peasants. True, it was not the first time in living memory that the state decided to reorganize the structure of peasant agriculture in the name of progress and social betterment … But no previous state reform had been conducted so violently and coercively. **❞**
>
> Sheila Fitzpatrick, *Stalin's Peasants: Resistance and Survival in the Russian Village*

Continuing to work on culture, Fitzpatrick introduced the discussion of the 1920s and Stalinism* as a cultural transformation rather than just a time of political and social change. She drew attention not only to the changing makeup of ruling society, but also the values they held—first those of revolutionary class* transformation (the abolition of social class as it had defined pre-Revolution Russia),* and then of conservatism, which they adopted in an attempt to defend their new gains.[2] The ultimate result, in the 1990s, was *Everyday Stalinism*, and a related, earlier work (*Stalin's Peasants: Resistance and Survival in the Russian Village*) that focused on the rural peasantry rather than urban citizens. Fitzpatrick combined and drew on her previous work in writing *Everyday Stalinism*, investigating the values and life experiences of a physically and socially mobile population that was being bombarded with images of class war and a utopian* socialist* future.

Integration

This work reflects Fitzpatrick's calls in the 1980s to differentiate society from the state more closely. She argued that when society was seen in terms of categories, they were always those defined by the state (peasants, workers, and so on). She never, however, argued that we must completely ignore the state—only that we should not see it as controlling all social interactions.[3] *Everyday Stalinism* takes up this challenge, examining how people dealt with regime-imposed categories. It also investigates how people interacted not only with the bureaucracy, but also with each other in the fields of work, shopping, and family. It anticipates her later work, in the 2000s, on how citizens created new identities and presented themselves at a time of revolutionary change. These arguments are also present in *Everyday Stalinism*, especially in its discussion of denunciations.*

Accordingly, this book can be seen both as a reflection of her previous thought and as a model for subsequent work; the latter continues its arguments and uses the same methodology, drawing heavily on the personal stories and experiences of ordinary Russians. She is currently furthering her interest in Soviet society by writing about ordinary people in the 1950s and 1960s, as well as expanding her interest in people's experience beyond Russia by studying displaced people within Germany.

Fitzpatrick's earlier works dealt with education policies, social mobility, and the widespread cultural changes that Stalinism brought about. In all of these, she was interested in how the experience of industrialization,* urbanization, and the utopian project of socialism affected the people involved, be they bureaucrats,* intellectuals, or citizens.

This core concept was more explicitly investigated in Fitzpatrick's previous work, *Stalin's Peasants.*[4] There she concentrated on the peasant masses that experienced Stalin's collectivization* campaigns (which saw individually owned and managed farms combined and then managed by the state), again focusing on how the state intervened in their lives and what strategies they used to survive. The same questions about the limits of Soviet power, and the divisions that it created through its campaigns, apply to both the peasants and the urban citizens that are the subject of *Everyday Stalinism*.

Significance

As both a leading light of revisionism and as an author who called on others to take the state out of the picture as much as possible, Fitzpatrick has remained a prominent figure in Soviet studies. Her early attention to social and cultural history, at a time when geopolitical* concerns (roughly, matters of international relations) and totalitarian models* dominated the field, inspired many of the scholars she herself later cited in *Everyday Stalinism*. Fitzpatrick opened up research into totalitarian societies, where previously there had only been the study of totalitarian states. Her innovations in the field, and her career-long attention to oral history, mass media, and popular culture, remain both extremely revealing of aspects of life in the USSR and an inspiration for others' research.

Everyday Stalinism was widely praised for its research and accessibility, with some noting that it is the starting point for much more research into the everyday spheres she explored.[5]   Her penetration of the political sphere to look at the impact of economics and propaganda* on everyday culture and social interactions has been recognized even by her critics, and testifies to the book's importance for the field.

NOTES

1   Sheila Fitzpatrick, *The Commissariat of Enlightenment. Soviet Organization of Education and the Arts under Lunacharsky, 1917–1921* (Cambridge: Cambridge University Press, 1970), 1.

2   See Sheila Fitzpatrick, *The Cultural Front: Power and Culture in Revolutionary Russia* (Ithaca: Cornell University Press, 1992).

3   Sheila Fitzpatrick, "New Perspectives on Stalinism," *Russian Review* 45, no. 4 (1986): 357–73.

4   Sheila Fitzpatrick, *Stalin's Peasants: Resistance and Survival in the Russian Village after Collectivization* (New York: Oxford University Press, 1994).

5   Jeffrey Rossman, "Review of *Everyday Stalinism*," *Journal of Modern History* 73, no. 3 (September 2001): 722–4.

SECTION 3
IMPACT

MODULE 9
THE FIRST RESPONSES

KEY POINTS

- Fitzpatrick was criticized for ignoring work and class* in her analysis of life in the Soviet Union.*

- She incorporated class into her later writing, saying she did not intend to create a general theory of Soviet* daily life but, rather, to discuss the effect of modernization on private life.

- Ultimately, Fitzpatrick's social history* approach to the Soviet Union (rather than the grand strategy approach) has become dominant in the field.

Criticism

While influential and widely praised, Sheila Fitzpatrick's *Everyday Stalinism: Ordinary Life in Extraordinary Times: Soviet Russia in the 1930s* has been criticized in many respects. She has, for example, been challenged for her decision to downplay the world of work as a sphere of everyday life, on the grounds that work varies too much from profession to profession. Families are also different, however—and she feels comfortable making comparisons in this regard. Lewis Siegelbaum,* an American professor of Russian history, points out that there were many "structures and experiences" that "transcended occupational differences."[1] Indeed, Fitzpatrick ignores an area that would have occupied a large section of most people's day, especially in a regime that placed such a premium on labor. Yet she does look at the effects of work on everyday life (as in the case of drunken or uninvolved fathers), and at the increased importance of the workplace as a social site, because workers typically ate communally.

> ❝ The identity issue in early Soviet Russia focused strongly on social class ... Nevertheless, the new rulers were sufficiently serious about class to undertake major statistical analyses of the class structure ... and also to put in place policies discriminating against 'class enemies.' ❞
>
> Sheila Fitzpatrick, *Tear Off The Masks! Identity and Imposture in Twentieth-Century Russia*

So while the social influence of work is not completely ignored, it is nevertheless downplayed.

Related to this is a stronger criticism—that Fitzpatrick ignores class as a category of analysis. The Ukrainian professor Serhy Yekelchuk* takes up this criticism forcefully, arguing that Soviet citizens did not live in a classless world, and that Stalinism* created new inequalities based on an individual's relation to the state.[2]

Responses

Although Fitzpatrick has not directly responded to any of the comments made about *Everyday Stalinism*, her reaction can be traced through interviews and her subsequent work. First, she states that she aimed to write a nontheoretical work, in which the evidence would speak for itself, rather than to represent a theory.[3] Scholars of the USSR* often talk about modernity and a modernizing project, as that is what the communists* themselves were consciously trying to achieve. Yet Fitzpatrick was more interested in the differences between this modernizing state and the private person. Her concerns are social history* and the aspects of personal life that resist analysis according to theories that draw on long-term historical trends or political models. She has offered a more traditional class-oriented analysis in her later works, and has demonstrated that she has always taken class seriously throughout her career.

In her subsequent book, *Tear Off The Masks! Identity and Imposture in Twentieth-Century Russia*[4] (2005), she examines the role of class more explicitly. She draws attention to the Bolsheviks'* obsession with social origin; they saw people's current social position as less important than the position they were born into, with the consequence that people were prompted to create their own, favorable, class identities. In effect, this investigation into class grows out of work already present in *Everyday Stalinism*, with regard to both self-fashioning and the importance of patronage.*

Neither the criticisms nor her response, which has not constituted a direct answer to any criticism in particular, point to a modification of Fitzpatrick's views. Instead, *Everyday Stalinism* must be seen as a work that expresses her research interests, which are often not those of her reviewers. "Class," too, is an imprecise term; Fitzpatrick is not interested in applying traditional Marxist* analysis to her research, preferring to look at why individuals do what they do. "Marxism" here refers to the social and economic analysis of the German political philosopher Karl Marx,* according to which the struggle between social classes is an especially important factor in the movement of history.

Conflict and Consensus

The opening up of new archives following the dissolution of the Soviet Union in 1991 and the subsequent work of scholars on the state's social history, of which Sheila Fitzpatrick's *Everyday Stalinism* is a key example, have fundamentally shifted the questions that are now asked in Soviet studies.

The concern of older academics with decision-making at the highest level of the regime, and questions such as the true numbers who died as a result of economic and social policies (such as the collectivization* of farms), have now diminished with the disappearance of the USSR as a geopolitical* rival to the West.* Fitzpatrick and younger scholars influenced by her revisionist* history have now moved the focus to questions of experience and consent, of how the regime's utopian* plans and actual shortcomings influenced identities and actions on the ground. There are a vast number of documents that can be studied, which continue to fuel research along the lines of *Everyday Stalinism* and to analyze the most significant factors that influenced modern life, such as economy, family, childcare, and friendship.

NOTES

1   Lewis H. Siegelbaum, "Review of *Everyday Stalinism*," *Slavic Review* 58, no. 4 (1999): 921.

2   Serhy Yekelchuk, "Review of *Everyday Stalinism*," *Journal of Ukrainian Studies* 26 (2001): 362.

3   Johan Öberg, "Sheila Fitzpatrick: A Leading Lady in Soviet Studies," *Baltic Worlds* 1 (2012): 4–10.

4   Sheila Fitzpatrick *Tear Off The Masks! Identity and Imposture in Twentieth-Century Russia* (Princeton: Princeton University Press 2005).

MODULE 10
THE EVOLVING DEBATE

KEY POINTS

- *Everyday Stalinism* has encouraged a trend toward looking at society independently of politics (that is, as something affected by, but not merely a product of, the state).

- While there is no Fitzpatrick "school of thought" as such, her research methods and her breadth of interest in Soviet* society has inspired much work in the area.

- Fitzpatrick has supervised many students who are now leading the field of Soviet studies.

Uses and Problems

Sheila Fitzpatrick's *Everyday Stalinism: Ordinary Life in Extraordinary Times: Soviet Russia in the 1930s* continues to be an important text for historians studying the Soviet Union.* In an overview of the field in 2007, the historian Mark Edele* argues that the "everyday" has replaced "society" in discussions of the contrast between state and society.[1] Fitzpatrick's terms have, then, not only become commonplace in the field but have driven new researchers to re-examine what they mean by "society," partly as a reaction to her own discussion of the "everyday."[2] More, her treatment of the paternalistic* Soviet regime, according to which society is more than just the product of the state, has become the benchmark by which new studies are carried out, despite its controversial nature.

Post-Soviet revisionist* analyses such as *Everyday Stalinism* and the work of the US historian Stephen Kotkin* now have their critics, but the current debate has been profoundly shaped by the terms and contrasts proposed by them. Insights about the everyday have been strongest in the

❝ The study of 'society' was replaced with the study of 'everyday life.' In what amounts to a social history with the structure left out, historians focus on everyday practices rather than on large-scale structures such as classes or society at large, as the 'old' social history had done. The one over-arching structure left in such analyses is the state ... [but] the state is only one element of the larger social organization that forms the context for everyday life and is in turn reproduced by it. ❞

Mark Edele, "Soviet Society, Social Structure, and Everyday Life"

studies of communism,* but have pointed to new directions for the study of other totalitarian* regimes, such as Nazi Germany.*[3] Fitzpatrick's insistence that there are many more spheres of Soviet life left to be explored has also been taken up by other scholars; for example, the experience of childhood is now coming under investigation.[4]

Schools of Thought

Sheila Fitzpatrick's work as a revisionist scholar in general and in *Everyday Stalinism* in particular has influenced a wide range of studies that are important in their own right. Her own students have taken up research of many aspects of everyday life that she first covered in this book. Without imposing her own view on her students, Fitzpatrick has also been influential in her methodology (her method of research and analysis), insisting that students proceed from "empirical* novelty to the available theory rather than the other way around."[5] "Empirical" here refers to evidence verifiable by observation; simply put, theories can be useful, but must be modified if the available data contradicts them.[6] While others have argued differently,[7] Fitzpatrick's influence can be felt through her inspirational breadth of interest and study of different aspects of the USSR.*

Everyday Stalinism itself has a number of direct descendants, notably the work of the historians Golfo Alexopoulos* and Julie Hessler.* Alexopoulos investigates the "social aliens" (those disenfranchised by Stalinism)* discussed in chapter 5 of *Everyday Stalinism,* looking at petitions sent to officials to describe how these excluded people changed their self-presentation in order to regain some of their rights.[8] She also follows the methodology of Fitzpatrick, who based a large part of *Everyday Stalinism* on local archives in the city of Smolensk. Alexopoulos found a previously unused cache of documents in a small Siberian town, which testified to thousands of citizens regaining rights by praising labor as a redeeming action, and by using traditional models of pleading based on Russian folk songs.

Hessler, on the other hand, investigates the black market* and shifts in consumption under Stalinism, again inspired by and informing Fitzpatrick's own work.[9] She also demonstrates that the state was actually, ideologically and at the highest level, opposed to the level of bureaucracy* and the shortages it created. Hessler notes the potential in Fitzpatrick's and her own work for comparison to other times and places, looking at how Soviet consumption models grew out of their imitation of German economic planning during World War I.*

Fitzpatrick's breadth of study has opened up many previously unexplored areas of Soviet history. These scholars and others have traded breadth for depth, probing further into subjects that Fitzpatrick explored briefly.

In Current Scholarship

As a graduate supervisor at the University of Texas, University of Chicago, and currently at the University of Sydney, Sheila Fitzpatrick has overseen a large number of Soviet-related doctorate students; in many ways they can be seen as her disciples. They focus on a diverse range of topics: Terry Martin* on nationalities policies; Julie Hessler on trade and consumer culture; Golfo Alexopoulos on social aliens; Yuri Slezkine* on state policies toward the small tribes of the north; and Roger Reese* on military history. The variety of her students' interests reflects her own career, which has rarely concentrated on one area for more than a single work. So one of Fitzpatrick's main influences has been to foster curiosity toward all aspects of Soviet history and society.

Her disciples have, then, modified and extended lines of argument started in *Everyday Stalinism,* and have used these ideas to explore other written histories; they have drawn inspiration from her methodology and, in finding meaning in every social action and sphere, have become influential in Soviet studies in their own right. Some are now influential professors themselves, holding Russian and Soviet history chairs at universities including Harvard (Martin) and University of California, Berkeley (Slezkine).

NOTES

1   Mark Edele, "Soviet Society, Social Structure, and Everyday Life: Major Frameworks Reconsidered," *Kritika: Explorations in Russian and Eurasian History* 8, no. 2 (2007): 349–51.

2   An important work is Jochen Hellbeck's work on Soviet diaries and subjectivity in *Revolution on My Mind: Writing a Diary Under Stalin* (Cambridge: Harvard University Press, 2006).

3   Nicholas Stargardt, *Witnesses of War: Children's Lives under the Nazis* (New York: Oxford University Press, 2005); Eric Johnson, *What We Knew: Terror, Mass Murder, and Everyday Life in Nazi Germany* (Cambridge: Basic Books, 2005).

4   Catriona Kelly, *Children's World: Growing Up in Russia 1880–1991* (New Haven: Yale University Press, 2007).

5   Jonathan Bone et al., "Roundtable: What Is a School? Is There a Fitzpatrick School of Soviet History?" *Acta Slavica Iaponica* 24 (2007): 233.

6   Bone, "What is a School?," 230.

7 For example, Bone et al, "What Is a School?".

8 Golfo Alexopoulos, *Stalin's Outcasts: Aliens, Citizens and the Soviet State 1926–1936* (Ithaca: Cornell University Press, 2003).

9 Julie Hessler, *A Social History of Soviet Trade: Trade Policy, Retail Practices, and Consumption 1917–1953* (Princeton: Princeton University Press, 2004).

MODULE 11
IMPACT AND INFLUENCE TODAY

KEY POINTS

- Fitzpatrick's *Everyday Stalinism* remains influential in its understanding that Soviet* society was more than just a creation of the state.

- Fitzpatrick's later work continues to oppose the totalitarian model* for understanding Soviet society.

- The American historian John Lewis Gaddis* is another major advocate of a more social and personal view of the USSR,* contrary to the abstract, political, totalitarian model.*

Position

The debate about the differences between state and society in the study of the Soviet Union* cannot be said to have started with Sheila Fitzpatrick's *Everyday Stalinism: Ordinary Life in Extraordinary Times: Soviet Russia in the 1930s*. Fitzpatrick was, however, influential in calling for "taking the state out of" studies of society as early as the late 1980s, when there was a debate among revisionists* about how to deal with the fact that the existing scholarship on Soviet society focused almost entirely on the state. Her work in the 1990s, of which *Everyday Stalinism* is the prime example, has shaped Soviet historiography's* approach to the question. The German-born historian Mark Edele* concludes his 2007 overview of the field with the statement that scholars are now seeing "the state [as] only one of the structural forms that constitute society."[1]

In *Everyday Stalinism*, Fitzpatrick defines the "everyday" as "everyday interactions that in some way involve the state."[2] What remains unclear, however, is the border between the state and society,

> **"**As ... stories about the late 1980s suggest, the
> system's collapse had been profoundly unexpected and
> unimaginable to many Soviet people until it happened,
> and yet, it quickly appeared perfectly logical and exciting
> when it began. **"**
>
> Alexei Yurchak, *Everything Was Forever Until It Was No More*

when the former is so heavily involved in the latter. This is also a pertinent question in democratic* states, which penetrate their societies through social programs and economic planning; this allows Soviet historians to enter into debate with other scholars, rather than seeing the Soviet experience as completely unique.

Everyday Stalinism is a prime example of post-1991 research. Because of the collapse of the Soviet Union that year, researchers benefited from a wealth of additional sources, and from the reduced pressure to write politicized history. The research agenda today is largely that of the revisionists, of which Fitzpatrick is arguably the most prominent. Her work has become a model for the types of topics young scholars research, such as education, the bureaucracy,* peasants, and workers' experiences. Her influence is not only felt through her well-received and much-cited books, but also through her role as supervisor to many young scholars, such as Golfo Alexopoulos* and Terry Martin.* Fitzpatrick's interest in the everyday and in the formation of identity, and her insistence that these were as much a part of the Soviet experience as the policymaking committee known as the Politburo,* has had a deep impact on the field today.

Interaction

Fitzpatrick's claims have driven debates on the nature of society in the Soviet totalitarian* regime, and on the extent to which we can take the state out of such an investigation. Her work in this book suggests that the state created both the field in which social interactions played out and the rules, which could be subverted or taken advantage of through networks of patronage.* While this view has been criticized by some, as it does not conform to Fitzpatrick's own 1980s view that the state needs to be left out, it has remained hugely influential and an unavoidable topic in any new history of the regime.

Fitzpatrick's interest in an all-encompassing "everyday" experience, away from a focus on work, the family, or gender (the sum of attributes used to define identities such as "male" or "female," and so on), has inspired other scholars to take the sphere of "ordinary life" as a topic with serious ramifications within totalitarianism. It has therefore helped to bring society and popular culture to bear on seemingly political questions, such as the fall of the USSR, and to encourage a dialogue between the disciplines of history and other social sciences,* especially anthropology* (the study of human cultures, beliefs, and society) and sociology* (the study of the functioning of society and social behavior).[3]

The Continuing Debate

With the downfall of the USSR in 1991, use of the totalitarian model in explanations of Soviet history lost power, given that it was associated with the needs of the West* in its struggle with communism.* The end of the USSR reduced the model's relevance and dampened any attempts to respond to the revisionist challenge. Some scholars who were prominent during the Cold War,* however, such as the historian John Lewis Gaddis,* have sought to move beyond the struggle between the totalitarian model and revisionism, in a movement that has been called "post-revisionist."*[4] Concerned with the geopolitical* question of who was to blame for the start of the Cold War, Gaddis has used the opening up of the Soviet archives to argue that while both sides had some responsibility, Soviet paranoia and distrust were the key drivers.

The "post-revisionist challenge" to revisionism was thought to involve "a move from social history,* which is relatively innocent of overt theory, to theory-driven cultural history. Fitzpatrick, who aimed to present the evidence without high-flown theoretical assumptions, is not entirely sure that post-revisionism's challenge has been successful.[5] The totalitarian model still retains its supporters—the Polish American Richard Pipes,* for example, a Soviet historian, still argues that the Russian Revolution* was an assault by an evil few on the lives of many Russians (making a similar point to that of the German American political theorist Carl Friedrich).*[6] This model was widely criticized throughout the twentieth century as narrowly political, being less concerned with accuracy than with making the Soviet Union, the West's Cold War rival, look bad. These challenges, however, are toward revisionism as a whole rather than Fitzpatrick in particular, and concern themselves mostly with old topics of diplomatic and political history rather than the social history exemplified in *Everyday Stalinism*.

NOTES

1   Mark Edele, "Soviet Society, Social Structure, and Everyday Life: Major Frameworks Reconsidered," *Kritika: Explorations in Russian and Eurasian History* 8, no. 2 (2007): 372–3.

2   Sheila Fitzpatrick, *Everyday Stalinism: Ordinary Life in Extraordinary Times: Soviet Russia in the 1930s* (New York: Oxford University Press, 1999), 3.

3   For a good example of this new type of social history, looking at the daunting political question of what caused the fall of the USSR, see Alexei Yurchak, *Everything Was Forever Until It Was No More: The Last Soviet Generation* (Princeton: Princeton University Press, 2005).

4   See John Lewis Gaddis, *We Now Know: Rethinking Cold War History* (Oxford: Clarendon Press, 1997).

5   Sheila Fitzpatrick, "Revisionism in Soviet History," *History and Theory* 46, no. 4 (2007): 87.

6   Richard Pipes, *The Russian Revolution* (London: Collins Harvill, 1990).

MODULE 12
WHERE NEXT?

KEY POINTS

- *Everyday Stalinism* is important for inspiring other work; its core concepts of both the Soviet* citizen in particular, and life in totalitarian* states in general, will continue to be influential.

- Students such as the Russian American historian Yuri Slezkine* and the American historian Terry Martin continue to look at the USSR* as a unique society rather than simply a state in which coercion and terror played a defining role.

- *Everyday Stalinism* argued that the Soviet citizen (*Homo Sovieticus*)* was forced to navigate a complex, mismanaged economy through risk-taking, favor trading, and patronage,* and that this profoundly influenced his or her identity.

Potential

Sheila Fitzpatrick's *Everyday Stalinism: Ordinary Life in Extraordinary Times: Soviet Russia in the 1930s* will continue to be relevant. The persistence of totalitarian regimes creates an ongoing need to understand how everyday life proceeds within them—especially as the relationship between state and society remains a fruitful area of inquiry. The category of "society" has often been replaced with the less conventional "everyday" in some studies—a testament to the enduring influence of a work that has shaped the vocabulary of the current debate. Its perceived shortcomings, including its dismissal of social class* as a category for historical analysis, have also spurred further research. In many ways, the continuing focus on social history* and cultural history can be attributed to the breadth of *Everyday Stalinism*,

> **❝** Today it is simply impossible for anyone seriously interested in Soviet history not to know and not to have read Sheila [Fitzpatrick]'s work, and our understanding of Stalinism in particular would be deeply impoverished without her contributions. **❞**
>
> Ronald Grigor Suny, in *Writing the Stalin Era: Sheila Fitzpatrick and Soviet Historiography*

whose chapters and sections offer a roadmap for the investigation of many spheres of everyday life.

Some of the book's other concepts, which have drawn less attention, may also be developed further. Most important is Fitzpatrick's description of the Soviet citizen as a risk-taker; this has implications for a supposedly rational and planned society that have not yet been fully explored. This area awaits further study, probably drawing on other, non-Soviet, work on risk. Fitzpatrick's statement that the "everyday" can be understood as "everyday interactions that in some way involve the state" has come in for much criticism, partly because it seems to run counter to her own, earlier calls to leave the state out of the discussion. This tension remains an indispensable part of the debate. Indeed, the picture she paints of the relation between state and society under Stalinism*—the state as a provider and setter of rules, and society as the set of interactions that play out according to the rules—has retained its influence. Much subsequent research has, to some extent, taken this as either a theoretical framework or a starting point for exploration.

Future Directions

Sheila Fitzpatrick's influence can be felt, through her own work and that of her students, in disciplines beyond Soviet studies. Her interest in the classics of theory, such as the nineteenth-century political philosopher Karl Marx's* influential work *Kapital* ("Capital"), has helped some of her students to develop their studies into areas beyond social history, carrying her influence and concerns into different disciplines. For example, the historian Yuri Slezkine's study of Soviet policies toward northern peoples in Russia introduced Fitzpatrick's concern with state interactions to anthropologists.* Another of her former students, Terry Martin, is a leading light in the development of a theory of neotraditionalism as a framework for understanding Soviet history—a school of thought that, while recognizing the USSR as a modernizing force, focuses on the old-fashioned institutions of its rule, such as patronage* and paternalism,* or its obsession with social categories.

Such theories have been influential in rethinking the nature of other totalitarian* regimes. Studies of both the USSR and Nazi Germany* have tended to focus on violence and coercion, but the shift toward looking at what citizens are thinking and how they react to state intervention has created a natural overlap between scholars of both regimes. The end of the USSR has removed the political value of comparing Soviet and Nazi regimes, and has paved the way for more scholarly comparisons, more of which are sure to come.

Summary

Sheila Fitzpatrick's *Everyday Stalinism* is the product of a mature scholar who had the self-confidence and experience to attempt a wide-ranging survey of Soviet society at a time of rapid change. It demonstrated that the state's mismanagement of the economy, combined with its modernization drive, gave rise to conditions that shaped the Soviet citizen (*Homo Sovieticus*, in Fitzpatrick's coinage) into a risk-taking survivor, looked after by a paternalistic state that resembled a soup kitchen. It is the major work on Soviet urban life in the 1930s, which benefited from the opening up of archives to give a sweeping overview of a state that created the conditions for new types of social interrelations. Its originality lay in its close attention to the existence of patronage networks, and in its dismissal of class* as a meaningful category for analysis.

Even more importantly, the book showed how all these forces created a discouraged but gambling population that was driven to depend on very close friends or patrons—despite living in a society pervaded by denunciations* and paranoia; in this society, citizens who still had agency (the capacity to act and change their circumstances) formed complex identities. The book decisively challenged notions of how people behave under totalitarianism. In treating all aspects of everyday life as meaningful for the formation of identity and society's development, from the smallest act of shopping to the bigger act of denouncing a neighbor, Fitzpatrick's text spurred an avalanche of studies on life in the USSR. Her key idea—that the search for a normal, comfortable life in a time of revolutionary change had a profound impact on people's expectations and mindsets—has served to provoke both new investigations and criticism.

GLOSSARY

GLOSSARY OF TERMS

Annales **school:** a French school of historical thought that emphasized the long-term influences on day-to-day living. This contrasted with the more traditional way of studying history, which presented dramatic events in sequence.

Anthropology: the study of human cultures, beliefs, and society.

Black market: an illegal market for goods.

Blat: a Russian term for trading favors or using influence for financial gain.

Bolshevik: the name of the dominant faction in the party that seized power in the Russian Revolution of 1917; it later became the Communist Party.

Bourgeois: a term used in the social analysis of Karl Marx to refer to the wealthy class that owns the means of production (for example, the owner of a shop, a factory, or any other business that produces goods or services).

Bureaucracy: the system of state or company administration, staffed by officials and civil servants. The word is often used to imply that the administration is too big, too complicated, too inflexible, or uncaring.

Capitalism: an economic system that emphasizes private property rights and the pursuit of profit from privately owned industry.

Civil liberties: freedoms for individuals that are protected from government interference. Free speech is an example of a civil liberty.

Class: the position held by people within society, defined by social stratification or their social position ("working class" or "middle class," for example).

Cold War (1947–91): a period of tension between the United States and the Soviet Union. The fear at the root of the Cold War came from the fact that each country had enough nuclear weapons to kill millions of the other's citizens. While the two countries never engaged in direct military conflict, they were involved in proxy wars, meaning they supported allied countries that fought each other.

Collectivization: from 1928, the Soviet policy of consolidating individual peasant farms and labor into collective farms, mostly by force.

Commissariat of Enlightenment: A bureaucracy established days after the Russian Revolution in 1917, overseeing education and the arts in a government committed to enlightening the people.

Communism: a political ideology that advocates state ownership of the means of production, the collectivization of labor, and the abolition of social class. It was the ideology of the Soviet Union (1917–91) and stood in contrast to free-market capitalism during the Cold War.

Democracy: a system of government in which the ruler or rulers of a state are elected by the people, who can also participate in government through other channels such as referendums.

Denunciation: the act of "exposing" (whether true or not) some other person as an undesirable or an enemy of the state.

Empirical: related to factual evidence, rather than theory.

Fascist Italy (1922–45): Italy as ruled by the dictator Benito Mussolini, which ruled on the basis of expansion of Italian territory and the institution of Italian nationalism.

Geopolitical: within the field of international relations, this describes the political system on a global scale; the intersection between politics and geography.

Great Leap Forward: a campaign by the Communist Party of China that ran from 1958 to 1961, intended to jumpstart China's industrialization and overtake Britain in production of steel and other products within 15 years. It led to millions of deaths from famine and state violence.

Great Terror (or Great Purge): Stalin's campaign of political repression that lasted from 1934 to 1939, and was particularly intense in 1937–8. Hundreds of thousands of people were executed, including high-ranking Communist Party members, military men, and peasants.

Harvard Project of Oral History: a project at Harvard University that aimed to present an oral history (a record of spoken narratives) of life in the Soviet Union, which has been expanded to other totalitarian states, including Iran.

Historiography: the academic discipline of how history is studied, and especially how different sources, techniques, and assumptions have been applied to different areas of study over time.

***Homo Sovieticus*:** "Soviet man;" a term invented by Sheila Fitzpatrick for the new communist citizen supposedly created by the state—

theoretically communal, scientific-minded, and building a communist future, but in practice subject to patronage and skilled in navigating bureaucracy and shortages.

Industrialization: The transformation from an agrarian to an industrial society through technological innovation and rapid economic growth, generally seen as starting with the Industrial Revolution in the late 1700s.

Magnitogorsk: a major industrial city in Russia.

Marxism: an intellectual school associated with Karl Marx and his followers, which holds that societies are split into classes that are inevitably in conflict with each other; that economic organization determines the way a society is ordered and ideas are formed; and that history progresses through stages, the final one of which will be a classless society.

Metaphor: a figure of speech, in which something is described by comparing it with something else that resembles it in some way.

Nazi Germany: the commonly used name for Germany between 1933 and 1945, when it was ruled by Adolf Hitler and the authoritarian and racist Nazi Party.

One-party state: a state with one political party. Other political parties and dissent are forbidden, and the distinction between the party and the state is often blurred.

Paternalism: an approach that aims to limit citizens' autonomy, supposedly for their own good.

Patronage: support or aid bestowed upon one person or group by another; a system defined by social inequality.

Politburo: the executive committee of a communist party. When capitalized, it normally refers to the Politburo of the Soviet Union.

Post-revisionism: in the field of history, the school of thought that emerged in the 2000s as a response to the revisionist focus on evidence rather than theory.

Propaganda: a form of state-centric communication that tries to affect how the population thinks.

Revisionism: the reinterpretation of orthodox views surrounding a particular historical period, often bringing new evidence to the subject or approaching it from a different angle (for example, Fitzpatrick approaches the Soviet Union from the viewpoint of citizens, rather than the state).

Russian Revolution (1917–21): a large-scale peasant rebellion against the traditional ruler of Russia (the Tsar) and the aristocracy. Following the Revolution, a communist government led by Vladimir Lenin took power.

Shortage economy: a term applied to centrally planned economies, in which the system inherently produces chronic shortages of consumer goods.

Social history: an approach to historical research and analysis in which the focus is on everyday men and women, and their experience of events, rather than the actions and motivations of monarchs, political leaders, statesmen, and so on.

Socialism: a political system in which the means of production (the tools and resources required by business and industry) are held in common ownership.

Social sciences: a blanket term for academic disciplines concerned with human society and social behavior, such as anthropology, economics, history, political science, and sociology.

Sociology: the study of the functioning of society and social behavior.

Soviet: originally referred to revolutionary councils set up by Russian workers in 1905 and 1917, but in later years came to refer to anything pertaining to the Soviet Union.

Sovietology: the academic school of study of the Soviet Union.

Soviet Ukraine: one of the 15 Soviet republics that existed between 1922 and 1991.

Soviet Union/Union of Soviet Socialist Republics (USSR): a superstate encompassing communist countries in Europe and Central Asia, with its capital in Moscow. Founded in 1922, it dissolved with the end of the Cold War in 1991.

Stalinism: the political ideology associated with Joseph Stalin, focusing on rapid industrialization, collectivized agriculture, and building socialism in one country rather than spreading a world revolution. The term is also synonymous with state violence and severe political repression.

State–society interaction: the relationship between the people and the state and its institutions.

Surveillance: the state of being watched or monitored by an authority.

Totalitarianism: a political system in which the state aims to exercise authority over society in every aspect, whether public or private. Often used to describe communist and fascist states.

Totalitarian model: a theory that holds that totalitarian states control every aspect of their citizens' public and private lives. Often used to draw comparisons between Nazi Germany, Fascist Italy, and the Soviet Union.

Utopia: a paradise, or otherwise perfect situation. The term also means an impossibly perfect place.

The West: broadly speaking, Europe and North America.

World War I: an international conflict from 1914 to 1918 centered in Europe and involving the major economic world powers of the day. The industrial advancements in military technology as well as the scale of the conflict resulted in vast military and civilian casualties.

World War II: a global conflict from 1939 to 1945 fought between the Allies (the United States, Britain, France, the Soviet Union, and others) and the Axis powers (Germany, Italy, Japan, and others). It was seen as a major moral struggle between freedom and tyranny, and included events such as the Holocaust, in which millions of Jews and others were killed by Nazi Germany.

PEOPLE MENTIONED IN THE TEXT

Golfo Alexopoulos is a professor at the University of South Florida whose first book, *Stalin's Outcasts*, focused on "social aliens" (those disenfranchised by Stalinism).

Zbigniew Brzezinski (b. 1928) is an American political scientist and strategist who has advised many US presidents on foreign policy.

Jimmy Carter (b. 1924) was president of the United States between 1977 and 1981.

Stephen F. Cohen (b. 1938) is an American historian, political scientist, and Russia specialist, who taught for many years at Princeton University.

Sarah Davies is an academic in Britain, at Durham University, focusing on Stalin's Russia.

Mark Edele is a German-born academic at the University of Western Australia specializing in the Soviet Union during the World War II era.

Lucien Febvre (1878–1956) was a French social historian and one of the fathers of the *Annales* school.

Brian Fitzpatrick (1905–65) was an Australian author and historian, and father of Sheila Fitzpatrick.

Carl Friedrich (1901–84) was a German American professor and political theorist.

John Lewis Gaddis (b. 1941) is professor of military history at Yale University and the most famous Cold War-focused historian in the West.

Wendy Goldman (b. 1956) is professor of history at Carnegie Mellon University in the United States, focusing especially on policies regarding daily necessities such as food.

Jochen Hellbeck (b. 1966) is professor of history at Rutgers University, focusing on identity formation in the Soviet Union, especially in relation to World War II.

Julie Hessler (b. 1966) is a historian of the Soviet Union at the University of Oregon, especially focusing on the black market.

Jürgen Kocka (b. 1941) is a German historian at the Social Science Research Center, Berlin. He is interested in how economic and technological change has formed what we might call "modern Europe."

Stephen Kotkin (b. 1959) is an American historian at Princeton University focusing on Russian studies. He also teaches on authoritarianism more generally.

Vladimir Lenin (1870–1924) was a Russian politician, intellectual, and revolutionary leader, instrumental in the Russian Revolution and the early Soviet government.

Moshe Lewin (1921–2010) was a Lithuanian scholar who lived and worked in the Soviet Union (including on collective farms) and worked primarily at the University of Pennsylvania. He was a major early revisionist social historian.

Anatoly Lunacharsky (1875–1933) was the Soviet people's commissar of enlightenment: a post established days after the Russian Revolution in 1917, with responsibility for education and the arts.

Roberta Manning (b. 1940) is an American historian at Boston College.

Terry Martin is a professor at Harvard University who has written extensively on Stalinism's nationalities policy and the creation of national identities.

Karl Marx (1818–83) was an enormously influential German philosopher and social scientist, the author of *Capital* and *The Communist Manifesto*. He was a founding thinker in the development of socialism and communism.

Roy Medvedev (b. 1925) is a Russian political writer and was a consultant to the Soviet government.

Elena Osokina (b. 1959) is a Russian scholar of trade and everyday life at the University of South Carolina.

Richard Pipes (b. 1923) is a Polish American academic who studies the Soviet Union, specializing in finding commonalities between the Soviets and the Nazis. He also worked for the American Central Intelligence Agency (CIA) to interpret Russian grand strategy.

Roger Reese is professor of history at Texas A&M University.

William Shakespeare (1564–1616) was an English playwright and poet, and is considered by many to be the greatest writer in the English language.

Lewis Siegelbaum (b. 1949) is professor of Russian history at Michigan State University, focusing on movement and migration.

Yuri Slezkine (b. 1956) is a Russian American historian at the University of California at Berkeley.

Joseph Stalin (1878–1953) was a high-ranking communist and the unchallenged leader of the USSR between 1928 and 1953.

Andrey Vlasov (1901–46) was a Red Army general who was captured by the Germans during World War II, and led an army of Soviet Prisoners of War against the USSR. Noted for its anti-Stalinist and anti-Soviet views, many members of his army tried to escape to the West once the war had ended.

Serhy Yekelchuk (b. 1966) is a Ukrainian professor of Germanic and Slavic studies at the University of Victoria.

WORKS CITED

WORKS CITED

Alexopoulos, Golfo. *Stalin's Outcasts: Aliens, Citizens and the Soviet State 1926–1936.* Ithaca: Cornell University Press, 2003.

Alexopoulos, Golfo, Julie Hessler, and Kiril Tomoff, eds. *Writing the Stalin Era: Sheila Fitzpatrick and Soviet Historiography.* New York: Palgrave Macmillan, 2011.

Bernstein, Peter L. *Against the Gods: The Remarkable Story of Risk.* New York: John Wiley & Sons, 1996.

Bone, Jonathan, Mark Edele, Matthew Lenoe, and Ron Suny. "Roundtable: What is a School? Is There a Fitzpatrick School of Soviet History?" *Acta Slavica Iaponica* 24 (2007): 229–41.

Cohen, Stephen F. *Rethinking the Soviet Experience: Politics and History Since 1917.* Oxford: Oxford University Press, 1985.

Edele, Mark. "Soviet Society, Social Structure, and Everyday Life: Major Frameworks Reconsidered." *Kritika: Explorations in Russian and Eurasian History* 8, no. 2 (Spring 2007): 349–73.

Fitzpatrick, Sheila. *The Commissariat of Enlightenment. Soviet Organization of Education and the Arts under Lunacharsky.* Cambridge: Cambridge University Press, 1970.

The Cultural Front: Power and Culture in Revolutionary Russia. Ithaca: Cornell University Press, 1992.

Everyday Stalinism: Ordinary Life in Extraordinary Times: Soviet Russia in the 1930s. New York: Oxford University Press, 1999.

"New Perspectives on Stalinism." *Russian Review* 45, no. 4 (1986): 357–73.

"Revisionism in Soviet History." *History and Theory* 46, no. 4 (2007): 77–91.

Stalin's Peasants: Resistance and Survival in the Russian Village after Collectivization. New York: Oxford University Press, 1994.

Tear Off The Masks! Identity and Imposture in Twentieth-Century Russia. Princeton: Princeton University Press, 2005.

Friedrich, Carl J. and Zbigniew Brzezinski. *Totalitarian Dictatorship and Autocracy.* New York: Frederick A. Praeger, 1968.

Gaddis, John Lewis. *We Now Know: Rethinking Cold War History.* Oxford: Clarendon Press, 1997.

Hellbeck, Jochen. *Revolution on My Mind: Writing a Diary Under Stalin.* Cambridge, MA: Harvard University Press, 2006.

Hessler, Julie. *A Social History of Soviet Trade: Trade Policy, Retail Practices, and Consumption 1917–1953.* Princeton: Princeton University Press, 2004.

Johnson, Eric and Karl-Heinz Reuband. *What We Knew: Terror, Mass Murder, and Everyday Life in Nazi Germany.* Cambridge: Basic Books 2005.

Kelly, Catriona. *Children's World: Growing Up in Russia 1880–1991.* New Haven: Yale University Press, 2007.

Kocka, Jürgen. *Industrial Culture and Bourgeois Society: Business, Labor, and Bureaucracy in Modern Germany.* New York: Berghahn Books, 1999.

Kotkin, Stephen. *Magnetic Mountain: Stalinism as Civilization.* Berkeley: University of California Press, 1997.

Lewin, Moshe. *Lenin's Last Struggle.* Translated by A. M. Sheridan Smith. Ann Arbor: The University of Michigan Press, 2005.

Manning, Roberta T. "Review of *Everyday Stalinism.*" *American Historical Review* 105, no. 5 (December 2000).

Öberg, Johan. "Sheila Fitzpatrick: A Leading Lady in Soviet Studies." *Baltic Worlds* 1 (2012): 4–10.

Osokina, Elena. *Hierarchy of Consumption: Life Under the Stalinist Rationing System 1928–1935.* Moscow: MGOU, 1993.

Pipes, Richard. *The Russian Revolution.* London: Collins Harvill, 1990.

Rossman, Jeffrey. "Review of *Everyday Stalinism.*" *Journal of Modern History* 73, no. 3 (September 2001): 722–4.

Siegelbaum, Lewis H. "Review of *Everyday Stalinism.*" *Slavic Review* 58, no. 4 (Winter 1999).

Slezkine, Yuri. *Arctic Mirrors: Russia and the Small Peoples of the North.* Ithaca: Cornell University Press, 1994.

Stargardt, Nicholas. *Witnesses of War: Children's Lives under the Nazis.* New York: Oxford University Press, 2005.

Yekelchuk, Serhy. "Review of *Everyday Stalinism.*" *Journal of Ukrainian Studies* 26, no. 1/2 (Summer 2001): 362.

Yurchak, Alexei. *Everything Was Forever Until It Was No More: The Last Soviet Generation.* Princeton: Princeton University Press, 2005.

THE MACAT LIBRARY
BY DISCIPLINE

AFRICANA STUDIES

Chinua Achebe's *An Image of Africa: Racism in Conrad's Heart of Darkness*
W. E. B. Du Bois's *The Souls of Black Folk*
Zora Neale Huston's *Characteristics of Negro Expression*
Martin Luther King Jr's *Why We Can't Wait*
Toni Morrison's *Playing in the Dark: Whiteness in the American Literary Imagination*

ANTHROPOLOGY

Arjun Appadurai's *Modernity at Large: Cultural Dimensions of Globalisation*
Philippe Ariès's *Centuries of Childhood*
Franz Boas's *Race, Language and Culture*
Kim Chan & Renée Mauborgne's *Blue Ocean Strategy*
Jared Diamond's *Guns, Germs & Steel: the Fate of Human Societies*
Jared Diamond's *Collapse: How Societies Choose to Fail or Survive*
E. E. Evans-Pritchard's *Witchcraft, Oracles and Magic Among the Azande*
James Ferguson's *The Anti-Politics Machine*
Clifford Geertz's *The Interpretation of Cultures*
David Graeber's *Debt: the First 5000 Years*
Karen Ho's *Liquidated: An Ethnography of Wall Street*
Geert Hofstede's *Culture's Consequences: Comparing Values, Behaviors, Institutes and Organizations across Nations*
Claude Lévi-Strauss's *Structural Anthropology*
Jay Macleod's *Ain't No Makin' It: Aspirations and Attainment in a Low-Income Neighborhood*
Saba Mahmood's *The Politics of Piety: The Islamic Revival and the Feminist Subject*
Marcel Mauss's *The Gift*

BUSINESS

Jean Lave & Etienne Wenger's *Situated Learning*
Theodore Levitt's *Marketing Myopia*
Burton G. Malkiel's *A Random Walk Down Wall Street*
Douglas McGregor's *The Human Side of Enterprise*
Michael Porter's *Competitive Strategy: Creating and Sustaining Superior Performance*
John Kotter's *Leading Change*
C. K. Prahalad & Gary Hamel's *The Core Competence of the Corporation*

CRIMINOLOGY

Michelle Alexander's *The New Jim Crow: Mass Incarceration in the Age of Colorblindness*
Michael R. Gottfredson & Travis Hirschi's *A General Theory of Crime*
Richard Herrnstein & Charles A. Murray's *The Bell Curve: Intelligence and Class Structure in American Life*
Elizabeth Loftus's *Eyewitness Testimony*
Jay Macleod's *Ain't No Makin' It: Aspirations and Attainment in a Low-Income Neighborhood*
Philip Zimbardo's *The Lucifer Effect*

ECONOMICS

Janet Abu-Lughod's *Before European Hegemony*
Ha-Joon Chang's *Kicking Away the Ladder*
David Brion Davis's *The Problem of Slavery in the Age of Revolution*
Milton Friedman's *The Role of Monetary Policy*
Milton Friedman's *Capitalism and Freedom*
David Graeber's *Debt: the First 5000 Years*
Friedrich Hayek's *The Road to Serfdom*
Karen Ho's *Liquidated: An Ethnography of Wall Street*

John Maynard Keynes's *The General Theory of Employment, Interest and Money*
Charles P. Kindleberger's *Manias, Panics and Crashes*
Robert Lucas's *Why Doesn't Capital Flow from Rich to Poor Countries?*
Burton G. Malkiel's *A Random Walk Down Wall Street*
Thomas Robert Malthus's *An Essay on the Principle of Population*
Karl Marx's *Capital*
Thomas Piketty's *Capital in the Twenty-First Century*
Amartya Sen's *Development as Freedom*
Adam Smith's *The Wealth of Nations*
Nassim Nicholas Taleb's *The Black Swan: The Impact of the Highly Improbable*
Amos Tversky's & Daniel Kahneman's *Judgment under Uncertainty: Heuristics and Biases*
Mahbub Ul Haq's *Reflections on Human Development*
Max Weber's *The Protestant Ethic and the Spirit of Capitalism*

FEMINISM AND GENDER STUDIES

Judith Butler's *Gender Trouble*
Simone De Beauvoir's *The Second Sex*
Michel Foucault's *History of Sexuality*
Betty Friedan's *The Feminine Mystique*
Saba Mahmood's *The Politics of Piety: The Islamic Revival and the Feminist Subjec*t
Joan Wallach Scott's *Gender and the Politics of History*
Mary Wollstonecraft's *A Vindication of the Rights of Women*
Virginia Woolf's *A Room of One's Own*

GEOGRAPHY

The Brundtland Report's *Our Common Future*
Rachel Carson's *Silent Spring*
Charles Darwin's *On the Origin of Species*
James Ferguson's *The Anti-Politics Machine*
Jane Jacobs's *The Death and Life of Great American Cities*
James Lovelock's *Gaia: A New Look at Life on Earth*
Amartya Sen's *Development as Freedom*
Mathis Wackernagel & William Rees's *Our Ecological Footprint*

HISTORY

Janet Abu-Lughod's *Before European Hegemony*
Benedict Anderson's *Imagined Communities*
Bernard Bailyn's *The Ideological Origins of the American Revolution*
Hanna Batatu's *The Old Social Classes And The Revolutionary Movements Of Iraq*
Christopher Browning's *Ordinary Men: Reserve Police Batallion 101 and the Final Solution in Poland*
Edmund Burke's *Reflections on the Revolution in France*
William Cronon's *Nature's Metropolis: Chicago And The Great West*
Alfred W. Crosby's *The Columbian Exchange*
Hamid Dabashi's *Iran: A People Interrupted*
David Brion Davis's *The Problem of Slavery in the Age of Revolution*
Nathalie Zemon Davis's *The Return of Martin Guerre*
Jared Diamond's *Guns, Germs & Steel: the Fate of Human Societies*
Frank Dikotter's *Mao's Great Famine*
John W Dower's *War Without Mercy: Race And Power In The Pacific War*
W. E. B. Du Bois's *The Souls of Black Folk*
Richard J. Evans's *In Defence of History*
Lucien Febvre's *The Problem of Unbelief in the 16th Century*
Sheila Fitzpatrick's *Everyday Stalinism*

Eric Foner's *Reconstruction: America's Unfinished Revolution, 1863-1877*
Michel Foucault's *Discipline and Punish*
Michel Foucault's *History of Sexuality*
Francis Fukuyama's *The End of History and the Last Man*
John Lewis Gaddis's *We Now Know: Rethinking Cold War History*
Ernest Gellner's *Nations and Nationalism*
Eugene Genovese's *Roll, Jordan, Roll: The World the Slaves Made*
Carlo Ginzburg's *The Night Battles*
Daniel Goldhagen's *Hitler's Willing Executioners*
Jack Goldstone's *Revolution and Rebellion in the Early Modern World*
Antonio Gramsci's *The Prison Notebooks*
Alexander Hamilton, John Jay & James Madison's *The Federalist Papers*
Christopher Hill's *The World Turned Upside Down*
Carole Hillenbrand's *The Crusades: Islamic Perspectives*
Thomas Hobbes's *Leviathan*
Eric Hobsbawm's *The Age Of Revolution*
John A. Hobson's *Imperialism: A Study*
Albert Hourani's *History of the Arab Peoples*
Samuel P. Huntington's *The Clash of Civilizations and the Remaking of World Order*
C. L. R. James's *The Black Jacobins*
Tony Judt's *Postwar: A History of Europe Since 1945*
Ernst Kantorowicz's *The King's Two Bodies: A Study in Medieval Political Theology*
Paul Kennedy's *The Rise and Fall of the Great Powers*
Ian Kershaw's *The "Hitler Myth": Image and Reality in the Third Reich*
John Maynard Keynes's *The General Theory of Employment, Interest and Money*
Charles P. Kindleberger's *Manias, Panics and Crashes*
Martin Luther King Jr's *Why We Can't Wait*
Henry Kissinger's *World Order: Reflections on the Character of Nations and the Course of History*
Thomas Kuhn's *The Structure of Scientific Revolutions*
Georges Lefebvre's *The Coming of the French Revolution*
John Locke's *Two Treatises of Government*
Niccolò Machiavelli's *The Prince*
Thomas Robert Malthus's *An Essay on the Principle of Population*
Mahmood Mamdani's *Citizen and Subject: Contemporary Africa And The Legacy Of Late Colonialism*
Karl Marx's *Capital*
Stanley Milgram's *Obedience to Authority*
John Stuart Mill's *On Liberty*
Thomas Paine's *Common Sense*
Thomas Paine's *Rights of Man*
Geoffrey Parker's *Global Crisis: War, Climate Change and Catastrophe in the Seventeenth Century*
Jonathan Riley-Smith's *The First Crusade and the Idea of Crusading*
Jean-Jacques Rousseau's *The Social Contract*
Joan Wallach Scott's *Gender and the Politics of History*
Theda Skocpol's *States and Social Revolutions*
Adam Smith's *The Wealth of Nations*
Timothy Snyder's *Bloodlands: Europe Between Hitler and Stalin*
Sun Tzu's *The Art of War*
Keith Thomas's *Religion and the Decline of Magic*
Thucydides's *The History of the Peloponnesian War*
Frederick Jackson Turner's *The Significance of the Frontier in American History*
Odd Arne Westad's *The Global Cold War: Third World Interventions And The Making Of Our Times*

LITERATURE

Chinua Achebe's *An Image of Africa: Racism in Conrad's Heart of Darkness*
Roland Barthes's *Mythologies*
Homi K. Bhabha's *The Location of Culture*
Judith Butler's *Gender Trouble*
Simone De Beauvoir's *The Second Sex*
Ferdinand De Saussure's *Course in General Linguistics*
T. S. Eliot's *The Sacred Wood: Essays on Poetry and Criticism*
Zora Neale Huston's *Characteristics of Negro Expression*
Toni Morrison's *Playing in the Dark: Whiteness in the American Literary Imagination*
Edward Said's *Orientalism*
Gayatri Chakravorty Spivak's *Can the Subaltern Speak?*
Mary Wollstonecraft's *A Vindication of the Rights of Women*
Virginia Woolf's *A Room of One's Own*

PHILOSOPHY

Elizabeth Anscombe's *Modern Moral Philosophy*
Hannah Arendt's *The Human Condition*
Aristotle's *Metaphysics*
Aristotle's *Nicomachean Ethics*
Edmund Gettier's *Is Justified True Belief Knowledge?*
Georg Wilhelm Friedrich Hegel's *Phenomenology of Spirit*
David Hume's *Dialogues Concerning Natural Religion*
David Hume's *The Enquiry for Human Understanding*
Immanuel Kant's *Religion within the Boundaries of Mere Reason*
Immanuel Kant's *Critique of Pure Reason*
Søren Kierkegaard's *The Sickness Unto Death*
Søren Kierkegaard's *Fear and Trembling*
C. S. Lewis's *The Abolition of Man*
Alasdair MacIntyre's *After Virtue*
Marcus Aurelius's *Meditations*
Friedrich Nietzsche's *On the Genealogy of Morality*
Friedrich Nietzsche's *Beyond Good and Evil*
Plato's *Republic*
Plato's *Symposium*
Jean-Jacques Rousseau's *The Social Contract*
Gilbert Ryle's *The Concept of Mind*
Baruch Spinoza's *Ethics*
Sun Tzu's *The Art of War*
Ludwig Wittgenstein's *Philosophical Investigations*

POLITICS

Benedict Anderson's *Imagined Communities*
Aristotle's *Politics*
Bernard Bailyn's *The Ideological Origins of the American Revolution*
Edmund Burke's *Reflections on the Revolution in France*
John C. Calhoun's *A Disquisition on Government*
Ha-Joon Chang's *Kicking Away the Ladder*
Hamid Dabashi's *Iran: A People Interrupted*
Hamid Dabashi's *Theology of Discontent: The Ideological Foundation of the Islamic Revolution in Iran*
Robert Dahl's *Democracy and its Critics*
Robert Dahl's *Who Governs?*
David Brion Davis's *The Problem of Slavery in the Age of Revolution*

The Macat Library By Discipline

Alexis De Tocqueville's *Democracy in America*
James Ferguson's *The Anti-Politics Machine*
Frank Dikotter's *Mao's Great Famine*
Sheila Fitzpatrick's *Everyday Stalinism*
Eric Foner's *Reconstruction: America's Unfinished Revolution, 1863-1877*
Milton Friedman's *Capitalism and Freedom*
Francis Fukuyama's *The End of History and the Last Man*
John Lewis Gaddis's *We Now Know: Rethinking Cold War History*
Ernest Gellner's *Nations and Nationalism*
David Graeber's *Debt: the First 5000 Years*
Antonio Gramsci's *The Prison Notebooks*
Alexander Hamilton, John Jay & James Madison's *The Federalist Papers*
Friedrich Hayek's *The Road to Serfdom*
Christopher Hill's *The World Turned Upside Down*
Thomas Hobbes's *Leviathan*
John A. Hobson's *Imperialism: A Study*
Samuel P. Huntington's *The Clash of Civilizations and the Remaking of World Order*
Tony Judt's *Postwar: A History of Europe Since 1945*
David C. Kang's *China Rising: Peace, Power and Order in East Asia*
Paul Kennedy's *The Rise and Fall of Great Powers*
Robert Keohane's *After Hegemony*
Martin Luther King Jr.'s *Why We Can't Wait*
Henry Kissinger's *World Order: Reflections on the Character of Nations and the Course of History*
John Locke's *Two Treatises of Government*
Niccolò Machiavelli's *The Prince*
Thomas Robert Malthus's *An Essay on the Principle of Population*
Mahmood Mamdani's *Citizen and Subject: Contemporary Africa And The Legacy Of Late Colonialism*
Karl Marx's *Capital*
John Stuart Mill's *On Liberty*
John Stuart Mill's *Utilitarianism*
Hans Morgenthau's *Politics Among Nations*
Thomas Paine's *Common Sense*
Thomas Paine's *Rights of Man*
Thomas Piketty's *Capital in the Twenty-First Century*
Robert D. Putman's *Bowling Alone*
John Rawls's *Theory of Justice*
Jean-Jacques Rousseau's *The Social Contract*
Theda Skocpol's *States and Social Revolutions*
Adam Smith's *The Wealth of Nations*
Sun Tzu's *The Art of War*
Henry David Thoreau's *Civil Disobedience*
Thucydides's *The History of the Peloponnesian War*
Kenneth Waltz's *Theory of International Politics*
Max Weber's *Politics as a Vocation*
Odd Arne Westad's *The Global Cold War: Third World Interventions And The Making Of Our Times*

POSTCOLONIAL STUDIES

Roland Barthes's *Mythologies*
Frantz Fanon's *Black Skin, White Masks*
Homi K. Bhabha's *The Location of Culture*
Gustavo Gutiérrez's *A Theology of Liberation*
Edward Said's *Orientalism*
Gayatri Chakravorty Spivak's *Can the Subaltern Speak?*

PSYCHOLOGY

Gordon Allport's *The Nature of Prejudice*
Alan Baddeley & Graham Hitch's *Aggression: A Social Learning Analysis*
Albert Bandura's *Aggression: A Social Learning Analysis*
Leon Festinger's *A Theory of Cognitive Dissonance*
Sigmund Freud's *The Interpretation of Dreams*
Betty Friedan's *The Feminine Mystique*
Michael R. Gottfredson & Travis Hirschi's *A General Theory of Crime*
Eric Hoffer's *The True Believer: Thoughts on the Nature of Mass Movements*
William James's *Principles of Psychology*
Elizabeth Loftus's *Eyewitness Testimony*
A. H. Maslow's *A Theory of Human Motivation*
Stanley Milgram's *Obedience to Authority*
Steven Pinker's *The Better Angels of Our Nature*
Oliver Sacks's *The Man Who Mistook His Wife For a Hat*
Richard Thaler & Cass Sunstein's *Nudge: Improving Decisions About Health, Wealth and Happiness*
Amos Tversky's *Judgment under Uncertainty: Heuristics and Biases*
Philip Zimbardo's *The Lucifer Effect*

SCIENCE

Rachel Carson's *Silent Spring*
William Cronon's *Nature's Metropolis: Chicago And The Great West*
Alfred W. Crosby's *The Columbian Exchange*
Charles Darwin's *On the Origin of Species*
Richard Dawkin's *The Selfish Gene*
Thomas Kuhn's *The Structure of Scientific Revolutions*
Geoffrey Parker's *Global Crisis: War, Climate Change and Catastrophe in the Seventeenth Century*
Mathis Wackernagel & William Rees's *Our Ecological Footprint*

SOCIOLOGY

Michelle Alexander's *The New Jim Crow: Mass Incarceration in the Age of Colorblindness*
Gordon Allport's *The Nature of Prejudice*
Albert Bandura's *Aggression: A Social Learning Analysis*
Hanna Batatu's *The Old Social Classes And The Revolutionary Movements Of Iraq*
Ha-Joon Chang's *Kicking Away the Ladder*
W. E. B. Du Bois's *The Souls of Black Folk*
Émile Durkheim's *On Suicide*
Frantz Fanon's *Black Skin, White Masks*
Frantz Fanon's *The Wretched of the Earth*
Eric Foner's *Reconstruction: America's Unfinished Revolution, 1863-1877*
Eugene Genovese's *Roll, Jordan, Roll: The World the Slaves Made*
Jack Goldstone's *Revolution and Rebellion in the Early Modern World*
Antonio Gramsci's *The Prison Notebooks*
Richard Herrnstein & Charles A Murray's *The Bell Curve: Intelligence and Class Structure in American Life*
Eric Hoffer's *The True Believer: Thoughts on the Nature of Mass Movements*
Jane Jacobs's *The Death and Life of Great American Cities*
Robert Lucas's *Why Doesn't Capital Flow from Rich to Poor Countries?*
Jay Macleod's *Ain't No Makin' It: Aspirations and Attainment in a Low Income Neighborhood*
Elaine May's *Homeward Bound: American Families in the Cold War Era*
Douglas McGregor's *The Human Side of Enterprise*
C. Wright Mills's *The Sociological Imagination*

Thomas Piketty's *Capital in the Twenty-First Century*
Robert D. Putman's *Bowling Alone*
David Riesman's *The Lonely Crowd: A Study of the Changing American Character*
Edward Said's *Orientalism*
Joan Wallach Scott's *Gender and the Politics of History*
Theda Skocpol's *States and Social Revolutions*
Max Weber's *The Protestant Ethic and the Spirit of Capitalism*

THEOLOGY

Augustine's *Confessions*
Benedict's *Rule of St Benedict*
Gustavo Gutiérrez's *A Theology of Liberation*
Carole Hillenbrand's *The Crusades: Islamic Perspectives*
David Hume's *Dialogues Concerning Natural Religion*
Immanuel Kant's *Religion within the Boundaries of Mere Reason*
Ernst Kantorowicz's *The King's Two Bodies: A Study in Medieval Political Theology*
Søren Kierkegaard's *The Sickness Unto Death*
C. S. Lewis's *The Abolition of Man*
Saba Mahmood's *The Politics of Piety: The Islamic Revival and the Feminist Subject*
Baruch Spinoza's *Ethics*
Keith Thomas's *Religion and the Decline of Magic*

COMING SOON

Chris Argyris's *The Individual and the Organisation*
Seyla Benhabib's *The Rights of Others*
Walter Benjamin's *The Work Of Art in the Age of Mechanical Reproduction*
John Berger's *Ways of Seeing*
Pierre Bourdieu's *Outline of a Theory of Practice*
Mary Douglas's *Purity and Danger*
Roland Dworkin's *Taking Rights Seriously*
James G. March's *Exploration and Exploitation in Organisational Learning*
Ikujiro Nonaka's *A Dynamic Theory of Organizational Knowledge Creation*
Griselda Pollock's *Vision and Difference*
Amartya Sen's *Inequality Re-Examined*
Susan Sontag's *On Photography*
Yasser Tabbaa's *The Transformation of Islamic Art*
Ludwig von Mises's *Theory of Money and Credit*